English Army Lists of the Early 1640s

Essential Civil War Series

English Army Lists of the Early 1640s

'Those Officers that are not mentioned in these Lists, have not as yet received their Commissions, by reason of their suddain imployment in the expedition.'
The List of the Army..., September 1642

Edited by S. F. Jones

Tyger's Head Books

Published by Tyger's Head Books

Copyright ©Tyger's Head Books, 2015

All rights reserved. No part of this publication may be reproduced, stored in a retrieval system or transmitted in any form or by any means whatsoever without the prior written permission of Tyger's Head Books.

Typeset in Adobe Caslon Pro
Typesetting and cover design by Tyger's Head Books
Printed by Lightning Source UK Ltd
ISBN 978-1-909596-05-4

Tyger's Head Books welcomes notice of errors in this volume.
See the website for information about our 'Bounty' system.

www.tygersheadbooks.co.uk
info@tygersheadbooks.co.uk

Contents

Editor's Note   7

The Bishops' War, 1640
[1] *A List of the Strength of the Kings Majesties Army, both Officers and Soldiers, as they were Mustered;* and *A List of the Colonels as also of the Severall Counties out of which they are to raise their Men; as also the Names of Ships, Captaines and Lieutenants that are now set forth...*
From 1640; published later by John Rushworth   9

Response to the Irish Rebellion of 1641
[2] *A List of the Field-Officers chosen and appointed for the Irish Expedition...*
June 1642; London   23

[3] *A List of the Names of Such Persons Who are thought fit for their accomodation, and the furtherance of the Service in Ireland...*
June 1642; London; a list of reformado officers to be retained   29

[4] *A List of his Majesties Navie Royall, and Merchants Ships*
December; London; probably a reprint of an earlier list   33

The First English Civil War, 1642
[5] *A Catalogue of the Names of the Lords that subscribed to Levie Horse to assist His Majestie.* Dated June, at York; printed July, at London   35

[6] *The List of the Armie...*
September; London; the first 'Parliamentarian' list   37

[7] *A Copy of the List of all the Cavaliers of his Majesties Marching Army...*
November; London   55

[8] *A Most True Relation of the Present State of His Majesties Army...*
December; London; derives from [7]   59

[9] *A Catalogue of the Names of the Dukes, Marquesses, Earles and Lords, that have Absented themselves from the Parliament, and are now with His Majestie*
December; London   65

[10] *A List of his Majesties Navie Royall, and Merchants Ships*
April 1643; London   67

Bibliography   71
Index   75

Abbreviations

BL – British Library
CSP – Calendar of State Papers
STC – (Pollard & Redgrave's) Short Title Catalogue
TT – Thomason Tracts (at the British Library)
'Wing' – Donald Wing's continuation of the Short Title Catalogue

Editor's Note

In the 1640s the somewhat bureaucratic English fancy for publishing what we would now call 'datasets' – almanacs, catalogues, indexes ('tables') and miscellaneous lists and collections of information of all types – collided with the Wars of the Three Kingdoms, and then the English Civil Wars. Printers were quick to issue detailed muster lists of the army and navy, which gave notice not only of the activities of the socially elevated great and good, but also their usually overlooked subordinates. Thus corporal of horse Bartholomew Johnson, whose name has survived if not his war record, enjoyed his fifteen minutes of fame just a few lines below the name of the Colonel General of the intended English expedition to Ireland in 1642; a 'master Stamford of Warwickshire', was noted as a cornet to the 'papist' Sir John Digby in December 1642, but given no further attention. Throughout the hostilities the details of hundreds of prisoners and casualties of war were similarly disseminated to the public. The passing eye of the fact-hungry press gave these men immortality in print and yet, an instant later, left them to obscurity; in that respect, perhaps little has changed over the intervening centuries. Undoubtedly, though, this was the first time their contributions were acknowledged *en masse* in public record for a wide audience.

The Lists
The purpose of this book is to untangle a number of military lists which were printed in the wake of the Bishops' War of 1640, the Irish rebellion in late 1641/early 1642, and the outbreak of the first English Civil War in 1642. Political chronicler John Rushworth published two muster lists for the 1640 expedition: the first names only senior officers and the numbers of men in their company; the second is more comprehensive but differs in vital detail such as the identity of colonels, the ranks of officers and the inclusion of six regiments not present earlier. The differences are such that they must represent details of the English force before and after the events at Newburn. They have been combined here as list [1], together with a third list giving purported strengths before the expedition, to give a full snapshot of the 1640 force. Equally as confusing is the June 1642 list for Ireland (list [2]): the names of many men known to have gone there do not appear on it, and some who were commissioned to go there did not take up their posts. The Lisle brothers from London are a case in point: according to *A Most True Relation* George Lisle 'had his Commission for a company in Ireland, but never came over', resurfacing at Edgehill in October on the King's side, whereas other sources reveal that his younger brother Francis certainly crossed to Ireland, serving there under Henry Warren until late 1643. However, neither brother is named in June and the details of their commissioning at that time is a mystery. Richard Willys, who became another prominent Royalist officer, was also named as an absentee 'Irish' recruit; he is not named in June either, and again reappears during the winter on the King's side. There were undoubtedly many similar cases. The printing of a second list in June (list [3]) adds to the noise: it contains the names of men retained by Parliament as reformado officers, ostensibly for Irish service but more likely in case

Parliament needed them to fight the King. This latter suggestion is supported by the sheer number of identifiable reformados whose names appear again in September on *The List of the Armie*, arguably the first appearance of Essex's 'Parliamentarian' army. The lack of more comprehensive information and further public lists, and the appearance of officers in places where they were not supposed to be points to a degree of bureaucratic confusion and a scramble by both King and Parliament to recruit, and by officers to be recruited or to avoid recruitment, according to their individual loyalties and circumstances.

A brief note must be made concerning lists [7] and [8]. The origin of the first, *A Copy of the List of all the Cavaliers of his Majesties Marching Army*, is an enigma as it bears little resemblance to the composition of the King's army in October 1642, as we presently understand it. The second, *A Most True Relation of the Present State of His Majesties Army*, uses [7] as its source and therefore includes manifest factual errors. Researchers should view both with extreme caution.

The title of this book, 'English Army Lists' is perhaps misleading, as it contains not only the names of cavalry, foot, and auxiliary land officers but also the officers of naval and merchant vessels assisting the King and / or Parliament between 1640 and 1643. The first modern writer to take notice of this mass of information was the antiquarian Edward Peacock, in *The Army Lists of the Roundheads and Cavaliers* in 1863 (it ran to a 2nd, revised edition in 1874). The only early list of his not included here is *A List of such English and Scotch Commanders, as have left their command under the Prince of Orange, from his leager at Rhineberk, with the names of each Captain's Garrison* (BL 669.f.6(66)), from August 1642. It includes a few officers who could be those named in English documents later that year, however the present editor could not view the original list in time for publication, therefore rather than include potential errors or omissions from Peacock's transcription, it has been omitted until a first-hand study can be made. Other documents included by Peacock but omitted here relate to clergy appointed to the Westminster Assembly, to Royalist Naseby prisoners and to Fairfax's army in 1647, but all of these are outside the scope of this book.

The Index

Entries are kept as simple as possible, at the minimum containing the individual's surname, first name, and page reference. Additional information such as rank, regiment and list date is only added where it is necessary to distinguish one officer from another, or to clarify which lists the man appears on. Occasionally, uncertainties concerning identity or possible list errors are also noted.

To avoid imposing unresearched assumptions onto the original lists, spellings have been kept strictly 'as is'; readers looking for a particular officer should consider alternative spellings. Pointers to these are included wherever possible. Where officers from different lists are indisputably, by virtue of an unusual name or well-known history, the same individual, their details are merged. Where the case is not so clear – for example, a June 1642 man appears to switch arm and rank by September, even perhaps dropping a rank – caution is exercised and the entries kept separate. Some names, for example Edward Gray, appear so many times across the lists that it is impossible to know how many individuals of that name are involved, and so all the entries are kept separate. In this respect the editor welcomes corrections and new information from other researchers.

[1]
A List of the Strength of the Kings Majesties Army, both Officers and Soldiers, as they were Mustered[1]

The Names of all the Collonels, Lieutenant Collonels, Sergeant Majors, Captaines, Lieutenants, Ensignes, Preachers, Chirurgeons, Quarter Masters, Provost Marshals under his Excellency the Earl of Northumberland, Captain General for this Expedition 1640. Taken according to the Muster Roll after the Armies Retreat from Newcastle into Yorkshire.

A List of the Colonels as also of the Severall Counties out of which they are to raise their Men[2]

I

Lord General [Algernon Percy, 10th Earl of Northumberland]
Troops levied in Hants (1200 men)

Northumberland	160
Lieutenant Colonel William Ashburnham	162
Serjeant Major Thomas Latham	93
Captain Charles Fludd/Lloyd[3]	103
Captain Henry Washington	95
Captain Jonathan Atkins	101
Captain Richard Dowse [D'Ewes?]	72
Captain Giles Porter [*later list only*]	
Captain James Chudleigh	108
Captain Sandford [*earlier list only*]	74
Captain Parramore [*earlier list only*]	92
Captain John Edwards	110
Captain George Hearne	_98_
	1268

Lieutenants: Guy Moulsworth; Lewis Gifford; John Tooley; Henry Chayton; William Moore; William Palmer; Barnaby Bradford; Edward Landen; Thomas Wylde;

---

[1] Rushworth, Second Part, pp.1241-1243. He includes two lists: the first only of officers ranked captain and above, together with the numbers of men they commanded; and the second a fuller list including junior officers and auxiliary staff but no numbers. Rushworth says of the first, that 'After the Arrival of the King's Army in the County of York, a Muster was taken thereof, which was as followeth'; whilst this does not explicitly state that the muster was taken on the new army's initial arrival in Yorkshire, the labelling of the second list as being post-retreat, and the numerous differences between the lists, strongly suggest that they were 'before' and 'after'. For clarity the lists are combined here. Peacock prints only the second one (pp.73-91).

[2] This is a single undated sheet, STC 19616, which gives only the colonels' names and the numbers of men to be levied from each county (above, these are the figures in italics immediately below the colonel's name). It is doubtful whether the intended numbers were ever raised. Additionally STC 19616 contains a navy list, which is included at the end of this section.

[3] The officer list says Fludd, the full list says Lloyd. 'Fludd' was probably a mis-hearing of 'Lloyd'.

Nathanael Dillon; Tristram Fenwicke; Roger Larrimore
Ensigns: John Newton; William Wentworth; Thomas Parrimore; Stephen Dawson; Charles Foster; Henry Miller; Robert Brandling; Robert Marsh; Edward Jackson; John Hilderson; John Salkeld; David Farrington
Preacher: Mr William Cox
Chirurgeon: Laurence Lowe
Quartermaster: Thomas Sandford
Provost Marshal: James Jeftres

II
Lord Newport, General of the Artillery
Troops levied in Gloucs. (1200 men)

Newport	163
Lieutenant Colonel George Moncke	125
Serjeant Major Henry Warren	112
Captain Thomas Sheldon/Shelton	95
Captain Postumus Kirten/Kirton	78
Captain Robert Croft[s]	83
Captain William Coape/Cope	78
Captain John Stradling	74
Captain Cashea Barrowes/Burrowes	93
Captain Henry Vanpeere	<u>77</u>
	0978

Lieutenants: George Lower; Arthur Moncke; Thomas Vaughan; Edmund Goffe; George Cooke; John Hoskins; John Weekes; James Gardiner; Owen Owens; Daniel Don
Ensigns: John Hamond; Richard Legg; John Fox; John Blunt; Thomas Paramore; Montague Sanderson; John Lutterell; John Washington; Edward Armory; Robert Bonny
Preacher: Higham Gibbs
Chirurgeon: Anthony Coquinx
Quartermaster: George Lawdy
Provost: John Parker

III
Sergeant Major General, Sir Jacob Ashley [Astley]
Troops levied in Oxon (600 men); Berks (500); Hants (100)

Astley	133
Lieutenant Colonel Sir Nicholas Selvin/Selwin	91
Serjeant Major Bernard Ashley [Astley]	99
Sr William Udall [Uvedale]	88
Captain James Baynton	101
Captain Robert Townsend	90
Captain Edward Ashley [Astley]	78

	[1]	
Captain St John[s]		90
Captain Robert Russell/Rushell		94
Captain William Bellasis/Bellowes		<u>88</u>
		0952

Lieutenants: William Lower; Michael Bedolph; Edward Fowles; George Slatford; Deverex Gibbons; John Haslewood; Isaac Cobb; Theodore Paleologus; Thomas Colbie; Henry Somerster.

Ensigns: Edward Courtney; Bray Knight; Francis Gay; Walter Neale; Peregrine Tasburgh; Hugh Pomeroy; Edward Nelson; Charles Thompson; ___ Oxford; George Fuller

Preacher: John Kowland
Chirurgeon: John Austin
Quartermaster: ___ Rawlins
Provost Marshal: Paul Knight

IV

Colonel George Goring
Troops levied in Northants (550 men); Rutland (60); Warks. (500); Leics. (90)

Goring	96
Lieutenant Colonel Thomas Kirke	99
Sergeant Major Richard Willis	97
Captain Edward Gray	87
Captain William Predeaux/Preddocks	66
Captain Charles Garrat/Gerrard	76
Captain Andrew Menns	48
Captain Thomas Danyell/Danil	89
Captain Henry Shelley/Sully	59
Captain Richard Elliot	<u>66</u>
	0783

Lieutenants: Richard Dowes; William Langon; William Swan; Henry Cooke; John Marly; Thomas Throgmorton; Robert Noyse; Francis Grover; Daniel More; Phillip Honywood

Ensigns: Richard Lovellis; Henry Crompton; ___ Warren; John Terwhit; John Millard; John Barbridge; Francis Lisle; Ralph Brandling; Joseph Brand; Arthur Chaune

Preacher: Richard Lloyde
Chirurgeon: [   ]
Quartermaster: Ben. Lawerowyes
Provost Marshal: Thomas Broxley

V

Lord Grandeson
Troops levied in Leics. (310 men); Worcs. (600); Gloucs. (290)

Grandison	172
Lieutenant Colonel Thomas Ballard	72
Sergeant Major Henry Sibthorp	106
Captain William Pretty	103
Captain Thomas Ellis	82
Captain George Lesley [Lisle/Lisley]	96
Captain John Boys	91
Captain Edward Villars [Villiers]	93
Captain Francis Smith	77
Captain Edward Varvay/Urney	<u>99</u>
	0996

Lieutenants: Thomas Browne, William Alford; John Malorye; William Smith; Robert Wiltshire; Robert Wynd; John Eaton; Daniel Broughton; Francis Gaudy; Phillip Ballard
Ensigns: John Bennet; John Carter; Hugh Justice; Henry Crooker; Henry Payton; Ralph Sparkes; Henry Marshin; John Cooney; John Walters
Preacher: Thomas Kent
Chirurgeon: John Earnlesse
Quartermaster: Phillip Cooke
Provost Marshal: Marmaduke Collins

VI

Lord Barramore [David, 1st Earl of Barrymore]
Troops levied in Pembrokeshire (300 men); Carmarthenshire (250); Glamorgan (200); Brecknockshire (200); Cardiganshire (150); Radnorshire (100)

Barrimore	181
Lieutenant Colonel Lawday [*earlier list only*]	169
Lieutenant Colonel Garret Barry [*later list only*]	
Sergeant Major James Usher	148
Captain Thomas Trafford	97
Captain Henry Bryan/O'Brian	95
Captain Gifford [*earlier list only*]	103
Captain Hemsley [*earlier list only*]	105
Captain Gray [*earlier list only*]	107
Captain Gwyn [*earlier list only*]	104
Captain Cary [*earlier list only*]	<u>105</u>
John Fitzgerald [*later list only*]	
Miles Power [*later list only*]	
George White [*later list only*]	
Charles Henise [*later list only*]	
Garret Parsell [*later list only*]	
	1214

Lieutenants: Daniel Bolton; David Barry; Richard Greatrix; Thomas Pheasant;

Lodowicke Price; Samuel Wright; William Weston; John Russell; Charles Stepkin; Richard Barry

Ensigns: William Barry; Phillip Barry; James Dallochin; John Barry; Nicholas Barry; Neptune Howard; James Bladwell; William Norcott; Robert Rosington; William Tomkins

Preacher: John Rocke
Chirurgion: Charles Oxenbridge
Quartermaster: Thomas Owens
Provost Marshal: John Baldwin

VII

Colonel Feilding [*earlier list only*][4]

Feilding	205
Arthur Aston [*later list only*]	
Lieutenant Colonel Richard Bol[l]e	160
Sergeant Major Robert Conisby/Coningsby	140
Captain Isaac Lukin[e]	98
Captain Richard Bradshaw	97
Captain Henry Kayes/Keyes	95
Captain Thomas Leighton	95
Captain Henry Thomas	96
Captain Thilwill [*earlier list only*]	95
Captain Apleton [*earlier list only*]	<u>92</u>
Captain William Courtney [*later list only*]	
Captain James Thomson [*later list only*]	
	1173

Lieutenants: Thomas Minn; William Keeling; Richard Spoore; William Roston; John Skipwith; Charles Hales; Celestine Bingham; Vul___ Wright; Nathanael Moyle; Stafford Sherborne

Ensigns: Francis Aston; Robert Bowles; Phillip Lowes; Robert Smith; John Atkins; James Browne; Robert Nelson; George Leigh; Richard Leigh; John Mynne

Preacher: Henry Jones
Chirurgeon: [   ]
Quartermaster: Lodowick Burwick
Provost Marshal: Tho. Goubourne

VIII

Colonel Henry Wentworth
Troops levied in Devon (1200 men)

Wentworth	191
Lieutenant Colonel Henry Wayte/Waite	135
Sergeant Major William Brockit/Brockett	134
Captain John Holman	89

---

[4] The regiment is not mentioned on the county levies list. 'Col. Feilding' must be Richard Feilding, as two officers, Thilwill and Apleton, also appear under 'Colonel Richard Feilding' on Rushworth's later list.

Captain Broichel Floyd/Lloyd	101
Sr Christopher Abdy	97
Captain Henry Fother[s]by	92
Captain Owen Parry	103
Captain Stanbury	94
Captain William Roberts	<u>103</u>
	1139

Lieutenants: Francis Kanyer; Frederick Windsor; Francis Boyer; Hugh Williams; Joseph Bamfeild; Robert Bingham; Gilbert Wheathill; John Higham; Thomas Stanbury; Robert Rookes
Ensigns: Edward Roberts; Isaac Throughton; John Thomas; Francis Smithwick; Humfrey Standburgh; William Lewis; Phillip Norris; Edmond Brockett; James Esline; Robert Herne
Preacher: Mr Matthew Whitley
Chirurgeon: Edward Hales
Quartermaster: William Bury
Provost Marshal: John Hodson

IX
Colonel Sir Thomas Glemham/Glenham
Troops levied in Wilts (200 men); Somerset (800); Bristol (200)

Glemham	212
Lieutenant Colonel Sir John Pawlet	166
Sergeant Major Robert Kirkby/Kirbie [*earlier list only*]	128
Sergeant Major Sir John Beaumont [*later list only*]	
Captain Robert Perkins/Pirkins	110
Captain George Wythers/Whither	101
Captain Story [*earlier list only*]	94
Captain Nicholas Cod[d]rington	103
Captain ___ Walgrave/Waldegrave	108
Captain Robert Mynn	98
Captain Thomas Dymmocke/Dymock	<u>91</u>
	1211

Lieutenants: John Waldegrave; William Pawlett; William Molineux; William Greene Jacob Stringer; Thomas Ward; James Bassett; Richard Norwood; William Neve
Ensigns: Edward Pereont; Thomas Pawlett; John Beamont; Theodore Delasley; Thomas Sanders; Hugh Gerrard; Francis Godfery; Arthur Ward; Henry Reyley
Preacher: [   ]
Chirurgeon: ___ Palmer
Quartermaster: William Moore
Provost Marshal: William Swaine

X

Sir John Merricke/Mirick
Troops levied in Staffs (300 men); Montgomeryshire (200); Hefs. (300); Monm. (250); Carnarvonshire (160)

Merrick	189
Lieutenant Colonel Thomas Carne	153
Sergeant Major William Davis	140
Captain Robert Broughton	94
Captain Edward Seymer/Seymore	92
Captain Thomas Button	97
Captain David Hide	103
Captain William Herbert	109
Captain Charles Skrimshawe/Shrumshaw	98
Captain William Maxie/May	<u>103</u>
	1177

Lieutenants: Thomas Langham; William Mathews; John Butler; Ambrose Tindall; John Edwards; William Mintridge; ___ Brase; ___ Waldwine; George Betts; John Lloyd
Ensigns: ___ Auberry; John Luther; William Owen; Thomas Smith; Thomas Cardinall; Gelly Merick; Miles Button; Thomas Milshaw; ___ Woods; Thomas Thwaytes
Preacher: Dr. Edward Alcaron [Alcorne]
Chirurgeon: [John Honyborne[5]]
Quartermaster: Henry Bishop
Provost Marshal: Isaac Chalise

XI

Sir Thomas Culpepper
Troops levied in Dorset (600 men); Devon (600)

Culpepper	160
Lieutenant Colonel Richard Gibson	90
Sergeant Major Ogle [*earlier list only*]	90
Sergeant Major Robert Turvill [*later list only*]	
Captain Walter Owen	81
Captain Lewis Lawkner [*later list only*]	
Captain Rowland St Leger/Sleger	90
Captain Roberts [*earlier list only*]	76
Captain Richard Thurland	94
Captain Francis Cooke	82
Captain Henry Boyer	88
Captain Nicholls [*earlier list only*]	<u>61</u>
Captain Samuel Payton [*later list only*]	

---

[5] Not mentioned in Rushworth's lists. Known from the State Papers of 25th March 1641, which record a wagon and horses being delivered to Honyborne and Dr. Alcorne, for the regiment's use (CSP Domestic Series, 1640-1641, p.513).

0912
Lieutenants: Daniell Nicholls; Compton Evers; John Sherman; Henry Ugall; William Mohun; Edward Louch; Richard Parker; Anthony Bushell; Anthony Thorpe; Richard Carter

Ensigns: Nicholas Lidcott; Thomas Lyster; John Chyne; Robert Goodwine; Peter Brewnett; John Steed; Lionell Beecher; ___ Bowdon; William Waldron; John Scanderith

Preacher: Edward Langford
Chirurgeon: [   ]
Quartermaster: William Weeler
Provost Marshal: ___ Turner

XII

Sir Charles Vavasour

Troops levied in Cheshire (500 men); [6] *Shrops. (500); Denbighshire (200)*

Vavasour	200
Lieutenant Colonel Tyrwhit [*earlier list only*]	155
Lieutenant Colonel Howard [*later list only*]	
Sergeant Major [Matthew] Apleyard	146
Captain Bascarvell [*later list only*]	
Captain Donnell/Doneill	108
Captain Scudamore	100
Captain Wynd/Winde	99
Captain Thornton/Therneton	109
Captain Pate	84
Captain Kinsmell/Kinsman	93
Captain Bridgeman [*earlier list only*]	<u>74</u>
	1163

Lieutenant: Thomas Bascarvell; William Evert; Phillip Hutton; Edward Dymmocke; Nathanael Smith; James Marwood; John Griffith; Edward Molworth; Jeremy Cheviers; George Masters

Ensigns: William Blakistone; Averoy Maleroy; Henry Chriswell; Richard Mason; Samuel Mallowes; Thomas Chapline; William Carre; Edward Cropley; John Holland; Giles Palmer

Preacher: Mr Thompson
Chirurgeon: ___ Bennett
Quartermaster: Rolland Davis
Provost Marshal: William Powell

XIII

Colonel William Vavasour

Troops levied in London (600 men); Cornwall (400); Devon (200)

---

[6] The State Papers record the raising of these Cheshire men, plus five drummers, on 4th July; they were 'raised, coated, and clothed ... at the expense of the county, and delivered ... to Sergeant Major Matthew Appleyard ...' (CSP Domestic Series, 1640, p.446).

[1]

Vavasour	101
Lieutenant Colonel Nicholas Mynn[e]	80
Sergeant Major Thomas Padgit/Pagett	74
Captain Charles Gillmore [*later list only*]	
Captain Edward Britt/Brett	62
Captain William Bedingfeild [*later list only*]	
Captain Lancelot Ho[u]ltby	60
Captain Nicholls	56
Captain Francis Leighton/Layton	56
Captain Henry Ferrer/Ferries	59
Captain Bowes [*earlier list only*]	60
Captain Baskavell [*earlier list only*]	62
Captain Maxwell [*earlier list only*]	<u>85</u>
	0755

Lieutenants: Robert Griffith; Ralph King; Francis Cowgrave; Owen Collugno; Nicholas Hughes; Francis Mills; John Wren; Robert Nicholas; Arthur Grant; Arthur Lowe

Ensign: Edward Chester; ___ Finch; Henry Baggett; Thomas Audey; Charles Fox; George Drewell; Fenix Wilson; Benjamin Brett; John Jefford; Robert Hugganes

Preacher: Mr Christian Sherwood

Chirurgeon: Trinity Langley

Quartermaster: Humfrey Farrew

Provost Marshal: [ ]

XIV
Colonel Thomas Lonsford [Lunsford]

Troops levied in Somerset (1200 men)

Lonsford	163
Lieutenant Colonel Henry Lonsford	71
Sergeant Major Gibbs [*earlier list only*]	72
Sergeant Major Powell [*later list only*]	
Captain Edward Powell	62
Captain Harbert Lonsford	87
Captain Hugh Pomeroy	84
Captain Francis Martin	75
Captain Dillon	61
Captain Thomas Capper/Cupper	68
Captain Edward Hippisley/Hippesley	<u>72</u>
	0815

Lieutenants: John Iremonger; Thomas Owen; John Sanbedge; Thomas Carrow; Ralph Lilley; Allen Povey; Poynton Castillion; Phillip Chalwell; Edward Hulstone; William Cheney

Ensigns: Titus Layton; Robert Skerrew; Edward Fowles; John Meredith; Pilemon

Sanders; William Atkins; William Bellow; Greevile Cary; John Cole
Preacher: [   ]
Chirurgion: [   ]
Quartermaster: Anthony Witherings
Provost Marshal: Elias Hickmar

XV

Sir William Ogle
Troops levied in Berks (100 men); Wilts (1100)

Ogle	175
Lieutenant Colonel Brutus Bucke	146
Sergeant Major Basset [*earlier list only*]	106
Sergeant Major Lawdey [*later list only*]	
Captain Constance Ferrer	70
Captain Edward Druryscuda [*later list only*]	44
Captain Edward Andrewes	44
Captain Henry Ventris	57
Captain Robert Sandys/Sandes	53
Captain Conyer Griffith/Griffen	59
Captain Cary [*earlier list only*]	64
Captain Fleetwood [*earlier list only*]	39
	0813

Lieutenants: ___ Fleetwood; Thomas Laward; Peter Gleane; Cornelius Ragan; George Lambert; Thomas Bennett; Charles Kirke; Edward Hackluyt; Thomas King; Francis Moore

Ensigns: Thomas Symoure; Edward Ogle; ___ Banard; Edward Maylard; Hugh Leigh; John Waite; William Andrewes; Gerrard Ogle; Hugh Gue; Robert Bacon

Preacher: Mr John Phillips
Chirurgeon: Henry Barker
Quartermaster: George Lisle
Provost Marshal: Thomas Bragge

XVI

Lord Marquess James Hamilton	211

Lieutenant Colonel Edward Feilding[7]
Troops levied in Norfolk (750 men); Suffolk (600 men); Cambs. (500)

Feilding	164
Serjeant Major John Berry	150
Captain Charles Dawson	110
Captain William Monyngs/Monnings	109
Captain Paul Smith	106
Captain Jervais Payne/Paine	106
Captain Francis Langley	107

---

[7] The county levies list puts the men under Feilding, not Hamilton.

Captain Peter Walthall	109
Captain Thomas Bozoone/Bosome	110
Captain Anthony Greve/Green	110
Captain Howard St John[s]	103
Captain Watson [*earlier list only*]	<u>108</u>
	1603

Lieutenants: Moses Treadwell; Emanuel Neale; William Denn; William Tuke; William Gualter; George Rouse; Godard Pemberton; Thomas Throughwood; George Little; Henry Bowerman; Henry Peto; John Wolverstone; Robert Watham
Ensigns: Bennett Prior; Henry Peters; Richard Cooke; Thomas Pergent; William Reevs; Walter Price; Anthony Williams; John Prenton; Thomas Best; Frances Willier; Thomas Carde; ___ Rogers; William Lane
Preacher: Mr. Deight
Chirurgion: Richard Smith
Quartermaster: John Daniell
Provost Marshal: Henry Fisher

The following six regiments are not present in the first muster list; the most likely explanation is that they were not present at York when the numbers were taken.

XVII

Colonel Sir Nicholas Biron
Troops levied in Derbys. (400 men); Notts (300); Lincs (200); Herts (500)
Lieutenant Colonel [   ]
Sergeant Major Edward Aldrich
Captains: John Watts; Thomas Sherley; John Middleton; Abraham Shipman; James Morgan; Roger Mollineux; Sheerly Shilling; Hercules Huncks; William Paterson
Lieutenants: Francis Stradling; Daniel Trever; Thomas Rush; John Marshall; Thomas Brumley; John Carnocke; Ralph Freeman; John Chonnocke; Edward Watts; Ithiell Luch; Thomas Garrett
Ensigns: Lambert Colield; Richard Bond; Michael Bland; John Exton; John Shipman; Daniel Redman; Christopher Elsing; John Elrington; George Hartrigg; Thomas May; Nicholas Watson; William Winter
Preacher: [   ]
Chirurgeon: [   ]
Quartermaster: Henry Bluder
Provost Marshal: John Fletcher

XVIII

Colonel Sir James Hamilton
Lieutenant Colonel John Slaughter[8]
Troops levied in Herts (150 men); Cambs. (50 men); Middx. (120)
Sergeant Major Francis Story

---
[8] The county levies list puts the men under Lt. Col. Slaughter, not Hamilton.

Captains: Thomas Dabscoate; Horatio Carew; Richard Munington; Thomas Gardiner; Thomas Cornewallis; Bullen Erreny; Anthony Brockett; Thomas Gifford; Thomas Thomas Bushell
Lieutenants: Thomas Rockwood; William Balyes; Roger May; John Andrews; John Grove; Duke Calton; William Corney; Thomas Townsend; Humfrey Corey; John Goodrich; Francis Poore; Thomas Bancks
Ensigns: John Blunt; John Heaslewood; Thomas Shelton; William Stratford; George Burwell; Isaac Wally; John Food; Thomas Leigh; Robert Bayles; John Lycent; Edward Purpitt; John Jervas
Preacher: Mr Henry Miller
Chirurgeon: [   ]
Quartermaster: William Dethick
Provost Marshal: William Richardson

XIX

Colonel Sir John Dougless
Lieutenant Colonel Sir Mathew Carry [Carew][9]
Troops levied in London (1200 men); Bucks (200)
Sergeant Major Arthur Basset
Captains: Sir John Le Hunt; Charles Ventress; Edward Kingstone; Thomas Middleton; James Barsey; James Powell; Robert Burghill; Nicholas Parker; George Windham
Lieutenants: Robert Gandey; Roger Hiddon; Samuel Kevison; Robert Davis; Thomas Ferrors; Robert Hamlon; William Gamblin; William Ross; James Cawardine; Thomas Andrewes; Thomas Draper; Robert Davyes
Ensigns: Thomas Kingstone; Silvanus Keyghtley; William Codrington; Michael Doughty; Humfrey Cornwall; Richard Naupham; George Carew; Thomas Carleton; Hugh Lovelace; Thomas Rookes; Edward Knightley; Thomas Coote
Preacher: Mr Humfry Sloconil
Chirurgeon: Clodius Adney
Quartermaster: Robert Juns
Provost Marshal: Richard Read

XX

Colonel Jerom Brett
Troops levied in Sussex (400 men); Surrey (800); Bucks (200)
Lieutenant Colonel Sir Vivian Molineux
Sergeant Major William Gibbs

Captains: Thomas Brett; Bartholomew Jukes; Stephen Hawkins; George Leake; Thomas Pettus; Henry Huddleston; John Godfrey; Digory Collins; Humfry Nicholls
Lieutenants: John Fisher; William Simpson; John Glassington; Francis Hooke; Robert Benbricke; John Palmer; John Clifton; Daniel Robinson; Nicholas Barnet; Nicholas Browne; Thomas Mollineaux; Giles Baskervill

---

[9] The county levies list puts the men under Carew, not Douglas.

Ensigns: Ambrose Jennings; Poole Turvill; Norrice Jepson; Thomas Hunt; Isaac Shawbury; Francis Bret; Thomas Birke; Francis Cobb; John Hunt; Roger Bendish; William Draper
Preacher: John Weld
Chirurgeon: [   ]
Quartermaster: William Bellamy
Provost Marshal: John Vittell

XXI
Colonel Francis Hamond
Troops levied in Sussex (200 men); Kent (700); Ci. Ports (300); Beds. (100); Bucks (100)
Lieutenant Colonel Robert Hamond
Sergeant Major: John Gifford
Captains: Mathew Gray; Edward Hamond; John Bayley; Arthur Roberts; James Ogle; Robert Ascough; Jeremy Manwood; Benjamin Eldred; Henry Mathewes
Lieutenants: Roger Burges; Thomas Conisby; Nicholas Deane; John Worsop; Daniel Goldsmith; Francis Whitney; Robert Scott; George Warson; Edward Tyerer; William Fisher; Christopher Crowe; Mathew Plowman
Ensigns: James Tooke; Richard Travers; ___ Walton; Edward Gray; Thomas Swinford; Henry Blundell; Ralph Murrian; Thomas Walkington; John Philpot; Henry Echlyn; ___ Plomer; John Fitzjames
Preacher: Henry Pike
Chirurgeon: [   ]
Quartermaster: Ferdinando Gray
Provost Marshal: Nicholas Knot

XXII
Colonel Richard Feilding
Troops levied in Essex (700 men); Hunts. (400); Beds. (300)
Lieutenant Colonel Francis Tirwhit
Sergeant Major Anthony Thelwell
Captains: Francis Tirringham; John Talbot; Thomas Collins; Toby Bowes; Edward Tirwhit; William Rolson; Robert Appleton; John Fox; Robert Barker
Lieutenants: Richard Oxenden; Denny Purvey; George Oakes; Salathiel Baxter; Thomas Hill; John Windfeild; John Errington; Edward Vincent; George Foord; John Cratroft; John Sutton
Ensigns: Francis Rogers; Henry Garfeild; Richard Francis; Edward Bray; Henry Hatcher; John Tirwhit; Foulke Woodroffe; Edward Disney; Charles Persall; Robert Ruston; ___ Cosworth
Preacher: William Beare
Chirurgeon: [   ]
Quartermaster: Walter Harcourt
Provost Marshal: Christopher Woodman

The names of Ships, Captaines, and Lieutenants

1. His Majesties Royall Shippe called the *James*, Sir John Pennington, Knight Admirall, and Captaine John Newcombe his Lieutenant.
2. His Majesties Ship called the *Charles*, Sir Henry Mainwaring, Knight, Vice-Admirall, and Master John Fauckner his Lieutenant.
3. His Majesties Ship called the *Swiftsure*, Captaine John Povey Rere-Admirall, and Captaine Thomas Turner his Lieutenant.
4. His Majesties Ship called the *Saint George*, Captaine John Morris Captain, and Captaine John Lure his Lieutenant.
5. His Majesties Ship called the *Rain-Bow*, Captaine David Murrey Captaine, and Master John Stansbey his Lieutenant.
6. His Majesties Ship called the *Garland*, Captaine John Fog Captaine, and Master Robert Fog his Lieutenant.
7. His Majesties Ship called the *Leopard*, Captaine Richard Swanley Cap. and Master William Smith his Lieutenant.
8. His Majesties Ship called the *Convertine*, Captaine Henry Stradling Captaine, and Master William Lutton his Lieutenant.
9. His Majesties Ship called the *Happy Entrance*, Captaine Robert Slingsbey Captaine, and Master Arthur Slingsbey his Lieutenant.
10. His Majesties Ship called the *Antelope*, Captaine Edward Popham Captaine, and Master John Darcey his Lieutenant.
11. His Majesties Ship called the *Mary Rose*, Captaine Thomas Price Captaine.
12. His Majesties Ship called the *Providence*, Captaine Philip Hill Captaine.
13. His Majesties Ship called the *Expedition*, Captaine Edmund Leaman Captaine.
14. His Majesties Pinace called the *Lions first Whelpe*, Captaine Ro. Fox Captaine.
15. His Majesties Pinace called the *Lions third Whelpe*, Captaine Thomas Braygrave Captaine.
16. His Majesties Pinace called the *Lions eighth Whelpe*, Captaine Anthony Woolward Captaine.
17. His Majesties Pinace called the *Lions tenth Whelpe*, Captaine Baldwin Wake Captaine.
18. His Majesties Ship called the *Greyhound*, Master Abraham Wheeler Captaine.
19. His Majesties Ship called the *Roe Bucke*, Master Thomas Rockwell Captaine.
20. His Majesties Ship called the *Nicodemus*, Master John Lambert Captaine.

[2]
A List of the Field-Officers chosen and appointed for the Irish Expedition...

Printed 11th Jun 1642, London (TT 669.f.6(31)); repr. 22nd Dec (TT E.64[4])

Troops of Horse

Colonel Generals Troop[10]
Captain Ralfe Whistler
Cornet Peter Ware
Quartermaster Nicholas Battersby
Corporals: Conyers Cooper; Bartholomew Johnson; Ralph Henery

Second Troop
Lord Broghill
Lieutenant John Allen
Cornet Cecil Ashcough
Quartermaster Thomas Hudson
Corporals: George Staples; Robert Bennet; Thomas Allen

Third Troop
Sir Faithfull Fortescue
Lieutenant Francis Doyet
Cornet Thomas Fortescue
Quartermaster Jo. Coyshe
Corporals: Jo. Vangerich, Jo. Marshall, Ralph Walcot

Fourth Troop
Lieutenant Colonel John Hurry
Lieutenant William Mercer
Cornet ___ Sedescue
Quartermaster Jo. Pearne
Corporals: Ralph Vickerman, Richard Whymper, William Crane

Fifth Troop
Alexander Nayrne
Lieutenant William Hyde
Cornet Marmaduke Cooper
Quartermaster Gedeon Lock
Corporals: Nathaniel Walmesley; Hugh Farr; Benjamin Ballard his ensign

---
[10] The Colonel General of the expedition was Philip, Lord Wharton.

Sixth Troop
John Trenchard
Lieutenant Adam Baynard
Cornet Jo. Hyde
Quartermaster Francis Fook
Corporals: Jo. Freake; Jo. Starkey; Thomas Gwalter

Seventh Troop
William St. Leger
Lieutenant Ed. Leventhorp
Cornet ___ Skrynsheere
Quartermaster Philip Vanderhiden
Corporals: Ed. Gray; Nicholas Phipp; Robert Wood

Foot Companies

Colonel General [Philip Wharton]
    His Captain, Edward Massy
    His Ensign, Oliver Cromwell
Lieutenant Colonel and Sergeant Major General Jeremy Horton
    His Lieutenant, Thomas Browne
    His Ensign, Ed. Greene
Sergeant Major, Owen Parry
    His Lieutenant, Ed. Browne
    His Ensign, Robert Hughes
First Captain, Vincent Calmady
    His Lieutenant, Edward Tyrer
    His Ensign, Richard Bland
Second Captain, Robert Long
    His Lieutenant, Thomas Allanby
    His Ensign, Roger Moore
Third Captain, Henry Carew
    His Lieutenant, Charles Holcroft
    His Ensign, William Heyden
Fourth Captain, Henry Skipwith
    His Lieutenant, Jo. Ivey
    His Ensign, Oliver St. John
Fifth Captain of Firelocks, Elias Struice
    His Lieutenant, Ed. Gray
    His Ensign, Thomas Barber

Second Colonel, Lord Kerrey
    His Captain, Robert Hamond
    His Ensign, Richard Bagot
Lieutenant Colonel, Henry Shelley

His Lieutenant, Jo. Ramsford
　　　His Ensign, Jo. Ashfield
Sergeant Major, Daniel Goodrick
　　　His Lieutenant, George Lower
　　　His Ensign, Charles Blount
First Captain, Charles Dawson
　　　His Lieutenant, Philip Meautas
　　　His Ensign, Jacob Stringer
Second Captain, Herbert Blankchard
　　　His Lieutenant, Morgan Tinney
　　　His Ensign, Chistopher Chudleigh
Third Captain, Agmondisham Muschamp
　　　His Lieutenant, William Dothwait
　　　His Ensign, Gervase Brach
Fourth Captain, Paul Wats
　　　His Lieutenant, Andrew Manwarring
　　　His Ensign, Thomas Barriffe
Fifth Captain for Firelocks, William Lower
　　　His Lieutenant, ___ Redman
　　　His Ensign, Jo. Raymond

Third Colonel, Thomas Ballard
　　　His Lieutenant, Thomas Grover
　　　His Ensign, Leonard Morton
Lieutenant Colonel, Sir Ed. Denny
　　　His Lieutenant, Ed. Odingsells
　　　His Ensign, William Garfoot
Sergeant Major, Francis Martin
　　　His Lieutenant, Robert Noyce
　　　His Ensign, Jo. Hardy
First Captain, Captain Primrose
　　　His Lieutenant, Edward Norbury
　　　His Ensign, William Fowlis
Second Captain, Edward Allen
　　　His Lieutenant, Francis Bower
　　　His Ensign, Robert Goodwin
Third Captain, Francis Fook
　　　His Lieutenant, Thomas Nayerne
　　　His Ensign, Henry Higgins
Fourth Captain, Thomas Middleton
　　　His Lieutenant, Jo. Lookar
　　　His Ensign, Charles Parker
Fifth Captain for Firelocks, Peter Nurford
　　　His Lieutenant, Robert Davis
　　　His Ensign, Henry Cope

Fourth Colonel, Charles Essex
    His Lieutenant, Francis Hall
    His Ensign, Jo. Shipman
Lieutenant Colonel, Adam Cunningham
    His Lieutenant, Peter Crispe
    His Ensign, Leonard Hawkins
Sergeant Major, Thomas Ogle
    His Lieutenant, James Webb
    His Ensign, Richard Osborne
First Captain, William Roberts
    His Lieutenant, Ambrose Tindall
    His Ensign, Jo. Watkins
Second Captain, George Narrow
    His Lieutenant, Edward Barnwell
    His Ensign, Thomas Paramour
Third Captain, Constance Ferrer
    His Lieutenant, William Hewet
    His Ensign, Jo. Hemings
Fourth Captain, Sam. Loftus
    His Lieutenant, James Barrell
    His Ensign, Francis Butler
Fifth Captain for Firelocks, John Jinkins
    His Lieutenant, Bartholomew Elecot
    His Ensign, Mr Wayte

Fifth Colonel, William Bamfield
    His Captain, Sam. Price
    His Ensign, ___ Caworth
Lieutenant Colonel, ___ Wagstaffe
    His Lieutenant, Thomas Coleby
    His Ensign, Robert Nelson
Sergeant Major, George Hutchinson
    His Lieutenant, Jo. Minshaw
    His Ensign, William Bourcher
First Captain, Jo. Bainfield
    His Lieutenant, Richard Bingley
    His Ensign, Ralph Garts
Second Captain, Horatio Carey
    His Lieutenant, Allen Povey
    His Ensign, Humfrey Burton
Third Captain, Robert Baker
    His Lieutenant, Michael Bland
    His Ensign, Jo. Rose
Fourth Captain, Christopher Burgh
    His Lieutenant, Thomas Hoare

His Ensign, Samuel Manaton
Fifth Captain for Firelocks, Rich Benson
    His Lieutenant, Thomas Latimer
    His Ensign, Jo. Browne

[3]
A List of the Names of Such Persons who are thought fit for their Accommodation, and the furtherance of the Service in Ireland, to be entertained as Reformadoes...

Printed 16th Jun 1642, London (TT 669.f.6(32))

Captains of Horse
William Pretty. James Wroughton. Thomas Temple. James Regnolds

Lieuetenants of Horse
Stephen Crow. Henry Sanderson. Richard Stevens. Joseph Cockain. William Anselme. Samuell Bossa. Troibus Turbervill.

Coronets of Horse
Henry Woodnorth. William Dowthwayte. John Degennes. Waynford. Nicholas Throgmorton

Coronets
William Baker. Chichester Phillips. Nicholas Shuttleworth. Randoll Cleyton. Joseph Jaques.

Quarter-Masters of Horse
Andrew Andrews. Arnold Haywood. Richard Stevens. Paul Scober. John Nelson. Richard Moore. Edward Maxwell. William Tovey. Henry Steward. Paul Gresham

Colonell of Foot
Henry Billingsley

Lieutenant Colonells of Foot
Sir Robert Winckfield. Edward Aldridge. Francis Clarke

Serjant-Majors of Foot
John Holeman. Thomas Dymocke. Edward Rowse.

Captains of Foot
Walter Ayleworth. Moyses Treswell. Sir Thomas Piggit. Francis Wilson. Jo. Drake. Jo. Powell. Jo. Errington. Antony Anderson. Thomas Laward. Walter Owen. Richard Carter. Thomas Rogers. Henry Crow. James Usher. Jo. Browne. Inde Leigh. Henry Ashley. Jo. Bayley. Thomas Bushell. Thomas Gaudy. Jo. Bolls. Jo: Waldegrave. Jo. Parkinson. George Welch. Francis Fairfax. Jo. Dillon. Thomas Bredman. Humphrey

Mathewes. George Purfoy. James Powell. Thomas Gilborne. Thomas Ward. Jo. Heigham. Henry Fotherby. George Lower. Sir William Fenton. William Butler. Oliver Wheeler. Sir John Leake. Francis Turner.

Colonell-Captains
Robert Hanson. Humphrey Cory. William Batters. Phillip Dutton. Edward Sanders. Theodore Palealogus. Prestland Molleneux. Richard Jones.

Lieuetenants of Foot
John Pollocke. Marmaduke Pudsey. Christopher Bingham. Francis Dingley. Thomas Lee. Jo. Balston. James Moore. Henry Ward. Jo. Robinson. John Flood. Jo. Bower. Theodore Willet. Robert Turner. Isaac Challice. William Cheney. Edward Watts. Roger Hidden. Robert Fennour. Henry Sommerstar. Jo. Exton. Osmond Williams, William Reston. William Spry. Titus Layton. William Cornay. John Marshall. Thomas Molleneux. Robert Wilsheere. George Phenix. Thomas Rush.

Colonell Ensigne of Foot
Robert Ludlowe. William Cowse

Captains Ensigns
Henry Bennett. Francis Jones. Jo. Clifton. Christopher Elsinge. Francis Fitzhughes. Anthony Masham. Edward Goodwin. Roger Walter. Jasper Brand. Edward Wood. Francis Rogers. Humphrey Dymocke. Thomas Dover. William Tucke. James Anderson. George Fulwood. James Ashley. Henry Blundell. Edward Johnson. Jo: Shancks. William Skipwith. Herald Gamble. Jo: Gratwicke. Ed. Hogedon. Thomas Button. Thomas Garret. Thomas Gwalter. Robert Blunt. Ellias Walley. Henry Mills. Robert Manly. Michael Cooke. Howard Kellet. Thomas Rookes. Lewis Pemberton. Jo: Wilsheere. Jo: Jervis. Jo: Licence. Walter Powell. Jo: Myn. Jo: Butrell. Hugh Justice. Jo: Hillersden. Richard Parker. Francis Bland. Roger West. Roger Willet. John Musgrave. Bartholomew Barns. Jo: Parris. Miles Hitchcocke.

Other Officers listed by the said Comittee
First Pay-Master of Horse and Foot, and all others that belongs to the Army, Nicholas Bond
His two Clerks; one of them to be employed in the Payment and keeping of Accompts for the trayn of Artillery.
Commissary of the Victuals of England, Walt. Frost
His Clerk.
Commissary of the fixed Magazine, Robert Goodwin
His Clarke, Richard Blatchford
Comisary of the victuals in the army, Geo. Downing
His Clerke, Hen. Griffith
Comisaries of the Muster, Sir Edw. Dodsworth

His Clerke, William Sherwood
Deputy Comisary of the Musters, Benil Predeux
His Clerke, Gregory Bland
Clerke of the Councel of War, Hen. Delamyne
One of the Physitians, Doctor John King
Apothecaries, Rich: Maning, Miles Raven
Controler of the Ordinance and chiefe Engineer, Philibert Eman. Duboyce.
Assistant to the Engineer, Anthony Outman
Gentlemen of the Ordinance, William Batters, John Jesopp, Thomas Vaines
Comisary of the Amunition, Thomas Crant
His Clerke, John Willet
Chiefe conductors of the amunition, draught horses and traine of Artillery, William Crawley
Under Conductors of the Amunition, and traine of Artillery, Edward Wase, Nicholas Gardiner, Edward Hunt
Battery Master and elder Mate to the Master Gunner, Edward Oakley
One Conductor of the Trenches, Christ. Richardson

The names of such as are not yet provided for this service
13 Chirurgions. 13 Chirurgions Mates. 1 Physitian. 4 Ministers. 1 Gunners Mate. 10 Canoneers. 1 Workmaster. 1 Conductor of the trenches. 3 Carpenters. 3 Wheelwrights. 1 Armorer. 1 servant to him. 1 Gunsmith. 2 Servants to him. 1 Stock-Master. 2 Servants to him. 1 Blacksmith. 1 Servant to him. 1 Farrier. 1 Servant to him. 1 Harnesse-maker. 1 Servant to him. 1 Cordmaker. 1 Servant to him.

Besides these
7 Smiths, to each troop one
7 Sadlers, to each troop one

As also some additions to the Colonell generals Regiments
Quartermaster generall, Hopton Haynes
Provost Master generall, Geo. Higham
Waggon Master Generall, Deverex Guibon

To the Lord Kerries regiment
Quartermaster, Zachary Walker
Provost Master, Richard Warburton
Waggin-master, Ralph Willins

To Colonell Ballards Regiment
Quarter-Master, William Rawlins
Provost-Master, Benjamin Ludlow
Waggon Master, Francis Gay

To Colonell Essex his Regiment
Quarter-Master, Christopher Crow
Provest-Master, Josua Sing
Waggon-Master, Simon Wheeler

To Colonell Banfeilds Regiment
Quarter-Master, Christopher Allenson
Provost-Master, Thomas Adama
Waggon-Master, Henry Beecher

[4]
A List of his Majesties Navie Royall, and Merchants Ships... [Dec 1642]

Printed 22ⁿᵈ Dec, London (TT E.64[4])

The Kings Majesties Ships: The Names of Captaines and Lieutenants, Ships, Men, and Burthens.

1. In the *James*, Robert Earle of Warwicke, Vice-Admirall, Master Slingsby Lieutenant, 260. men, burthen 875. tun.
2. In the *Saint George*, William Batten Captaine, Master William Smith Lieutenant, 260. men, burthen 792. tun.
3. In the *Raine-bow*, Sir John Menns Captaine, Master Lutten Lieutenant, 260. men, burthen 721. tun.
4. In the *Reformation*, Sir David Murrey Captaine, Master Standsbury Lieutenant, 260. men, burthen 731. tun.
5. *Victory*, Captaine Fogge Captaine, Master Fogge Lieutenant, 240. men, burthen 742. tun.
6. *Henrietta Maria*, Captaine Hatch Captaine, Master Wattes Lieutenant, 250. men, burthen 793.tun.
7. *Unicorne*, Captaine Frenchfield Captaine, Master Sommerston Lieutenant, 250. men, burthen 767. tun.
8. *Charles*, Swanley Captaine, Master Darey Lieutenant, 250. men, burthen 810 tun.
9. *Vanguard*, Captaine Blith Captaine, Master Blith Lieutenant, 250. men, burthen 751. tun.
10. *Entrance*, Captaine Owen Captaine, Master Bowen Lieutenant, 160. men, burthen 539. tun.
11. *Garland*, Captaine Slingsby Captaine, Master Walters Lieutenant, 170. men, burthen 767. tun.
12. *Lyon*, Captaine Prisse Captaine, Master Hill Lieutenant, 170. men, 602. tun.
13. *Antelope*, Captaine Burley Captaine, Master Willeby Lieutenant, 160. men, burthen 512. tun.
14. *Mary Rose*, Captaine Fox Captaine, 100. men, burthen 321. tun.
15. *Expedition*, Captaine Wake Captaine, 100. men, burthen 301. tun.
16. *Greyhound*, Captaine Wheler Captaine, 50. men, burthen 126. tun.

Merchants Ships
1. In the *Martane*, Captaine George Martaine Captaine, Master Hakriger, Lieutenant, 210. men, burthen 700. tun.

2. *Samson*, Captaine Ashly Captaine, Master Andrew Lieutenant, 180. men, burthen 600. tun.
3. *Caesar*, Captaine Elias Jorden Captaine, Master Norton Lieutenant, 180. men, burthen 600. tun.
4. *London*, Captaine John Stephens Captaine, Master Pomroy Lieutenant, 180. men, burthen 600. tun.
5. *Unicorne*, Captaine Edward Johnson Captaine, 143. men, burthen 475. tun.
6. *Mary Flower*, Captaine Peter Andrews Capaine, 121. men, burthen 450. tun.
7. *Bonny Venter*, Captaine George Swanly Captaine, 120. men, burthen 400. tun.
8. *The Prosperous*, Captaine William Driver Captaine, 120. men, burthen 400. tun.
9. *Hurclens*, Captaine Mover Captaine, 150. men, burthen 350. tun.
10. *Paragon*, Captaine Leonard Harris Captaine, 105. men, burthen 350. tun.
11. *Hopefull Luke*, Captaine Lee Captaine, 105. men, burthen 350. tun.
12. *Golden Angell*, Captaine Walker Captaine, 105. men, burthen 350. tun.
13. *Exchange*, Captaine Lucas Captaine, 89. men, burthen 325. tun.
14. *Mayden-head*, Captaine Lewton Captaine, 90. men, burthen 300. tun.
15. *Providence*, Captaine William Swandly Captaine, 81. men, burthen 271. tun.
16. *Jocelyn*, Captaine Partridge Captaine, 60. men, burthen 200. tun.

His Majesties Ships for the Irish Seas
1. The *Swallow*, Captaine Thomas Kettley, 150. men, 160. tun.
2. *Bonny Venture*, Captaine Henry Stradling, 160. men, 557. tun.

Merchants Ships
1. *Discovery*, Captaine John Brok-haven, 144. men, 380. tun.
2. *Ruth*, Captaine Robert Constable, 120. men, 400. tun.
3. *Employment*, Captaine Thomas Asly, 132. men., 440. tun.
4. *Peter*, Captaine Peter Stroung, 81. men, 270. tun.
5. *Pennington*, Captaine Joseph Jordan, 360. men, 135. tun.
6. *Fellowship*, Captaine Thomas Colle, 87. men, 290. tun.
7. *Mary*, Captaine William Capell, 30. men, 103. tun.
8. *John*, Captaine John Thomas, 15. men, 50. tun.

[5]
A catalogue of the names of the Lords that subscribed to levie horse to assist his majestie in defence of His Royall Person

List dated 22nd June 1642, York; printed 18th Jul (Wing N1033); repr. 22nd Dec, London (TT E.64[4])

Whereas it may be collected by severall Declarations printed in the name of both Houses of Parliament; That the Kings sacred person, the Houses of Parliament, the Protestant Religion, the Lawes of the Land, the Liberty and Propriety of the Subject, and Priviledges of Parliament are all in danger;

We whose names are under-written doe voluntarily offer and severally ingage our selves, according to the following Subscriptions, to assist his Majestie in defence of his Royall Person, the two Houses of Parliament, the Protestant Religion, the Lawes of the Land, the Liberty and Propriety of the Subject, and Priviledges of Parliament; when his Majestie shall have given Commission under Great Seale, for levying of Forces for those purposes, against all power, Levies and Forces whatsoever, or to be upon any pretence whatsoever;

To pay Horses for three Months, thirty dayes to the Month, at two shillings and six pence *per diem*, still advancing a Months pay, the first payment to begin so soone as the King shall call for it, after the Commissions shall be issued under the Great Seale. In this Number are not to be reckoned the Horses of the Subscribers, or those that shall attend them.

	Horse
The Prince	200
The Duke of Yorke	120
Lord Keeper	40
Duke of Richmond	100
Lord Marquesse Hertford	60
Lord Great Chamberlaine	30
Earle of Cumberland	50
Earle of Huntington	20
Earle of Bathe	50
Earle of Southampton	60
Earle of Dorset	60
Earle of Northampton	40
Earle of Devonshire	60
Earle of Dover	25
Earl of Cambridge	60

Earle of Bristoll	60
Earle of Westmerland	20
E. of Barkshire and L. Andover	30
Earle of Monmouth	30
Earle Rivers	30
Earle of Carnarvon	20
Earle of Newport	50
Lord Mowbray	50
Lord Willoughby	30
Lord Gray of Ruthin	10
Lord Lovelace	40
Lord Paget	30
Lord Faulconbridge to come	
Lord Rich	30
Lord Pawlet	40
Lord Newarke	30
Lord Mountague	30
Lord Coventrey	100
Lord Savill	50
Lord Mohun	20
Lord Dunsmore	40
Lord Seymor	20
Lord Capell	100
Lord Faulkland	20
Master Comptroller	20
Master Secretary Nicholas	20
Lord Chief Justice Banks	20

The Lord Thanet is not here, but one hath undertaken for 100. for him.
Sum total 1695

[6]
The List of the Armie

Printed 14th Sep 1642 (TT E.117[3]); repr. 22nd Dec (TT E.64[4])

The List of the severall Regiments of Foot and Horse

Officers generall of the Field
His Excellency Robert Earle of Essex, Captaine Generall.
Philip Skippon, Serjeant Major Generall, and President of the Councell of Warre.
Captaine James Seigneur Provost Marshall Generall.
Thomas Richardson Carriage Master Generall.

Officers of the Lord Generalls Train
Sir Gilbert Gerrard Knight, Treasurer at Warres.
Lionell Copley Esquire, Muster-Master Generall.
Doctour Isaack Dorisla, Advocate of the Army.
Henry Parker Esquire, Secretary to the Army.
Robert Chambers, Auditor of the Army.

Officers Generall of the Horse
William Earle of Bedford, Lord Generall.
Sir William Belfoore Knight, Lieutenant Generall.
John Dulbeir, Quarter-Master Generall.
Sir Edward Dodsworth, Commissary for the Horse.
John Ward, Commissary for the Provisions.
John Baldwine, Provost Marshall Generall.

A List of the Train of Artillery
John Earle of Peterborough, Generall of the Ordnance.
Philibert Emanuel de Boyes, Lieutenant Generall of the Ordnance.
Nicholas Cooke, an Assistant to the Lieutenant of the Ordnance.
Alexander Forboys, a Surveyor or Comptroller.
John Lyon, an Engineer.
Six other Engineers Assistants.
George Vernon, John Phipps, two Commissaries of the Ordnance, Materialls, and Ammunition.
A Commissary to distribute Victualls.
Captaine Peter Cannon, a Purveyor Generall, both for Munition and all other necessaries belonging to the Ordnance.

Eighteen Gentlemen of the Ordnance

1. Tho. Holyman.
2. Robert Barbar
3. Patrick Strelley
4. Edward Wase
5. Anthony Heyford
6. Robert Bower
7. Henry Edson
8. James Francklin
9. Richard Honey
10. Joshua Sing
11. George Ransom
12. Samuell Berry
13. Daniell Barwick
14. Tho. Rawson
15. Tho. Sippence
16. Tho. Crosse
17. Tho. Ayres
18. William Hickson

John Fowke, a Master of the Carriages, or Waggon-Master for the Artillery.
Wil. Crawley, a principall Conductor of the Train of Artillery for the Draught Horses and Ammunition.
Edward West, a Commissary of the Train of Artillery for the draught-Horses.
George Wentworth, a Quarter-Master of the Traine of Artillery.
Edward Frodsham, Henry Roe, John Dungan, three Captaines to 600. Pyoners.
Gerard Wright, Benjamin Hodson, Tho. Williams, three Lieutenants to 600. Pioners.
Lancelet Honiburne, Master-Gunner.
Christopher Troughton, Provost-Marshall of the Artillery.
Edward Okely, a Battery-Master.
Joakin Hane, Fire-worker and Petardier.
William Roberts, Fire-worker and Petardier.
Harman Browning, a Bridge-Master for the Train of Artillery.
Jo. Herdine, an Assistant unto him.
Lieutenant Generall De Boys Captaine of 100 Fire-locks.
Rich. Price, Lieutenant to Captain De Boys.

His Excellencies Regiment

Captaines	*Lieutenants*	*Ensignes*
Colonell his Excellency		John Lloyd
Lieu. Col. W. Davies	John Rainsford	Jenkin Song
Ser. M. Jo. Bamfield	Fulk Musket	
Sir Antho. St. John.	Hugh Justice	Edward Cockram
Chr. Mathias	Wal. Reed	Will. Bowen
Jo. Skrimpshiere	Geo. Clarke	
Tho. Skinner	Alex. Edwards	Jo. Johnson
Roger Bettridge	Jo. Cracroft	Tho. Hastings
Tho. Ward	Tho. Lanford	Andr. Ward
Edw. Leventhorp	Hen. Stevens	Hugh Harding

Sir Philip Stapleton Captain of 100. Curassiers for his Excellencies Guard, Adam Baynard Lieutenant, Paul Gresham Quarter-Master, Captain Nathaniel Draper Captain to the Generals Troop of 50. Carbines, John Strelley Cornet, Abraham Carter Quarter-Master.

Fire-Locks
Captains, Robert Turner, Ambrose Tindall, Nicholas Devereux
Physitian to the Train and Person, Doctor John Saint John
Chirurgion to the Traine and Person, Lawr. Lowe
Chirurgion to the Regiment, William Parkes
Lieuetenants, Useus Martery, Nich. Halford, Tho. Lawrence
Carriage-Master, William Wren
Chaplain, Stev. Marshall
Chaplain for the Regiment of Horse, Doctor Burges

Sir John Merricks Regiment

Captaines	*Lieutenants*	*Ensignes*
Col. Sir Joh. Merrick		
L. C. Vincent Kilmady		
Ser. M. Will. Herbert		
___ Tyer		
___ Lower		
Fran. Merrick		
Tho. Lawherne		
John Lloyd		
John Edwards		
John Baily		

Provost Marshall, John Treme
Chaplain, Tucker.
Chirurgion, John Woodward

The Earle of Peterboroughs Regiment

Captaines	*Lieutenants*	*Ensignes*
Col. Jo. E. of Peterborow.	Geo. Rouse	___ Goldsborow
L. C. Sir Faithf. Fortescue.	Richard Orfice	John Apew
S. M. Francis Fairfax	Jo. Rice	Alex. Thory
Sir Edw. Payton	William Thorp	John Bridges
Phil. Dutton	Henry Case	James Harrison
Bevill Prideaux	Ornall Fountaine	Bevill Cruttenden
Robert Knightley	Tho. Treist	Richard Lidcoat
Jo. Butler	John Balstone	Thomas Laharn
Hen. Lovell	George Hartridge	John Pewe
Geo. Blunt	James Grimes	Cha. Harrow

The Earle of Stamfords Regiment

Captaines	Lieutenants	Ensignes
Col. Hen. E. of Stamford	John Clifton	John Chambers
Lieu. Col. Edw. Massie	James Harcus	Jo. Starkey
Ser. M. Const. Ferrer	William Hewet	Tho. Griffin
Tho. Savill	William White	William Pincock
Edw. Gray	James Bock	James Gray
Charles Blunt	Robert Hampson	Hen. Collingwood
Peter Crispe	Jo. Hemens	Tho. Barnes
Isaac Dobson	Nath. Tapper	James Baker
Arnold Cosbie	Robert Mallery	Laur. Clifton
Jo. Bird	Hen. Cantrell	

Quarter-master, Ferdinando Gray
Carriage-master, Rich. Phillips
Chirurgion, Jo. Rice
Provost Marshall, Robert Powell

The Lord Sayes Regiment

Captaines	Lieutenants	Ensignes
Col. William Lord Say	John Rainsford	John Butcherfield
L. C. Geo. Hutchinson	Luke Weekins	Joseph Farnes
Ser. M. Ja. Atchason	Jam. Hannam	Jo. Kelly
Geo. Marrow		
Christo. Burgh	___ Hoare	___ Corby
Jam. Temple	___ Langford	Ben. Lee
Walter Lloyd	Tho. Haynes	Tho. Golledge
Morgan Tinne	William Howard	___ Gittings
Robert Blowe	Jon. Newcomin	Tho. Sweeper
Buffy [Bussy?] Basset	Edw. Carwardine	Prue Prideaux

Quarter-master, Hum. Dix.

The Lord Whartons Regiment

Captaines	Lieutenants	Ensignes
C. Phil. L. Wharton	Ch. Holcroft	___ Blake
Lieu. Col. Jer. Horton	Fr. Fitshues	Tho. Radford
Ser. Ma. Owen Parry	Edw. Browne	Robert Hughs
Robert Long	Tho. Albany	Roger Moore
Henry Carew	William Browne	William Heydon
Jude Leigh	William Bridges	Edw. Horton
Henry Skipwith	George Usher	Jo. Garret
Chr. Baily	William Emerson	Jer. Gardiner
___ Gibbons	Anthony Masham	Rich. Bland
Elias Struce	Isaac Turney	Edw. Horton

Provost Marshall, George Higham
Chirurgion, Jo. Broughton

The Lord Rochfords Regiment

Captaines	*Lieutenants*	*Ensignes*
Col. Lord Rochford	Jo. Norship	
Lieu. C. Ed. Aldrich	William Shawe	Henry Newdigate
Ser. Ma. Th. Leighton	Edw. Deering	Mount Sanders
Tho. Drake	Walter Bradley	Jeffery Lloyd
George Walsh	Ralph Carter	Peter Blewin
Philip Ballard	Edw. Melson	Edw. Lovell
Benjamin Hooke	Jo. Sheppard	George Burrell
Fran. Hudson	Matth. Stoaker	William Williams
Jasper Brand	Humphry Dimock	Hen. Smith
Geo. Willoughby.	Miles Ashton	Jo. Bramston

Quarter-master, Miles Dobson
Chaplain, Jo. Page
Provost Marshall, Jo. Burbeck
Carriage-master Jo. Poore

The Lord Saint-Johns Regiment [Oliver, 5th Baron St. John of Bletso]

Captaines	*Lieutenants*	*Ensignes*
Col. Oliver L. St. John	Theo. Paholigus	Jo. Marshall
Lieu. Col. Tho. Essex	Will Boughty	Tho. Joy
Ser. Ma. Ed. Andrews	William Casie	Edw. Gravenor
Timo. Neale	Jos. Sears	Geo. Elliot
Oliver Beecher	Lyon Pilkington	Lewis Mordent
Jo. Harvie	Tho. Bedealls	Noah Neale
Lewis Pemberton	Edw. Carew	Hen. Tayler
Tho. Miles	Rich. Moore	Jos. Scarborough
Jo. Hilderson	John Wood	Ric. Parker
Tho. Thorogood.	Wendy Oxford	Hen. Lovell

Carriage master, Tho. Greene
Quarter-master, William Walwin
Provost Marshall, Robert Lucas
Chaplain, Jo. Vinter
Chirurgion, William Roberts

The Lord Brooks Regiment

Captaines	*Lieutenants*	*Ensignes*
Col. The Lord Brook.	John Ashfield	John Davis
Lieu. Col. Sir Edw. Peto.	Christ. Langton	John Warren
S. M. Wal. Ailworth	Daniel Hinton	Tho. Roberts

Tho. Fitch	Nich. Ling	William Taton
Jo. Lilborne	John Mattersey	Tho. Hinde
Ralph Cotsforth	Jo. Morris	Hum. Lyeathcock
Tho. Hickman	Roger Cotterell	Jo. Peto
Nicho. Warren	John Gates	Tho. Ginnings
___ Sambridge	___ Wivell	___ Cotton
John Bridges	William Bridges	___ Eggleston

Waggon-master, John Smith
Quarter-master, John Hunt
Provost Marshall, William Coleman
Chirurgion, John Cleare

The Lord Mandeviles Regiment

Captaines	Lieutenants	Ensignes
Col. Hen. L. Mandevill	___ Turkington	
L. Col. Jo. Parkinson	John Hoskins	Jasper Goodwin
Ser. Ma. John Drake	Roger Whetstone	Nath. Walmsly
Fran. Wilson	Fra. Ballard	Tho. Davies
Hen. Samerster	Hen. Worth	Jo. Ramsey
Edw. Watts	Jo. Rose	Cha. Davies
Robert Goodwin	Bridges Bushell	Tho. Goodwin
Robert Palmer	Nich. Dibdale	Math. Milbourn
Dan. Redman	Hugh Beeston	___ Fleming
Osborn Williams	James Blodwell	John Daily

Provost-Marshall, John Turner
Carriage-master, Robert Ousby
Chaplain, Simon Ash
Quarter-master, Nich. Wood
Chirurgion, William Stannard

The Lord Roberts [Robartes] his Regiment

Captaines	Lieutenants	Ensignes
Col. John. L. Roberts		Tho. Rouse
L. Col. Will. Hunter	Geo. Graden	William Hender
Ser. M. Alex. Hurry	Tho. Keckwick	Alex. Tulidaffe
James Witcherly	Rich. Baron	Cuthbert Farley
John Walker	Walter Heys	Jos. Normington
Jo. Mercer	John Melvin	John Skudamore
Mark Grimes	Tho. Turrell	Mark Grimes
John Mill	Barnard Smelomb	Edw. Jenings
Jonath. Elliot	John Spooner	Ben. Groome
Jam. Fookes	Dan. Trevor	John Merrick

Quarter-master, William Rawlins
Provost Marshall, Hum. Franouth
Carriage master, Thom. Higgins
Chaplain, D. Calibut Downing
Chirurgion, Edw. Cooke

Colonel Cholmlies Regiment

Captaines	Lieutenants	Ensignes
Col. Sir He. Cholmly	Mich. Jobson	Hugh Philips
L. Col. Launce Alured	Mich. Dane	George Rotheram
Ser. M. Th. Southcot	William Wellin	Hen. Burksley
Henry Jenkins	George Fulwood	Tho. Apleby
William Bateler	Jo. Shanke	
Henry Katcose	Jo. Fisher	William West
Goddard Leigh	___ Andrewes	
Richard Jones	___ Goodwin	Barth. Burrell
Robert Hunt	Smith Wilkinson	Herald Skrimshaw
John Bury		

Provost Marshall, Nicholas Garth
Chaplain, Adoniram Bifield

Colonel Hollis his Regiment

Captaines	Lieutenants	Ensignes
Col. Denzell Hollis	Rich. Parker	Ralph Walset
L. C. Hen. Billingsley	Jo. Court	Rawley Willis
Ser. Maj. Jam. Quarls	Geo. Hampson	Edw. Neve
Allen Povey	Roger Noard	Tho. Cattorill
William Barke	Jo. Owen	
Richard Lacy	Tho. Lawrence	Robert Willoughby
George Harlocke	___ Samuel	Tho. Clement
Jo. Francis	Tho. Churchman	Alexander Payard
William Burles		
Bennet		

Colonel Bamfields Regiment

Captaines	Lieutenants	Ensignes
Col. Willm. Bamfield	Jo. Hart	Samson Manaton
L. C. Sr Ro. Wingfield	Ambr. Cade	George Wingfield
Ser. Major Sam. Price	Ralph Garth	Sym. Giggins
Robert Baker	Tho. Durdo	Jo. Rose
Richard Benson	Thomas Latimer	Jo. Browne
John Jesop	Hogan Rookwood	William Blake
Jo. Minshaw	Hum. Burton	Richard Jackson
William Owen	Albion Derickbore	Jo. Price

Thomas Staffarton
___ Pawlet

Hen. Wray
Andrew Ball

Fr. Barker
Tho. Hudson

Chaplain, ___ Freeman
Chirurgion, Richard Searle
Quarter-master, Chri. Allanson
Carriage-master, Hen. Beecher
Provost Marshall, Richard Gay

Colonel Granthams Regiment

Captaines	*Lieutenants*	*Ensignes*
Col. Tho. Grantham	Francis Gay	Nethermill Garrard
Lieu. C. Fran. Clarke	Edw. Tetlow	Tho. Browne
Ser. Ma. Jo. Holman	Isaac Challys	Thomas Coo
Hen. Ashley	Thomas Lee	George Langford
Sir Tho. Pigot	Steph. Deane	Jo. Middleton
Richard Gibbs	Edw. Apseley	Henry Gurney
Tho. Rogers	Jo. Blanden	Sheldon Napper
Francis Grantham	Miles Hitchcock	Job Throckmorton
George Slatford	Geo. Walter	Ben. Betsworth
Henry Blundell	Tho. Sparrow	Tho. Blundell

Quarter master, Hen. Throckmorton
Provost Marshall, Robert Gibbons
Carriage master, Jo. Hopkinson

Sir William Constables Regiment

Captaines	*Lieutenants*	*Ensignes*
Col. Sr. W. Constable	Edm. Hakluit	Joseph Smith
Lieu. Col. Rob. Grain	Jo. Linch	William Knight
Ser. M. He. Frodsham	___ Sumner	William Miller
Tho. Eure	Jo. Dugdaile	Arthur Young
Jam. Breckham	Tho. Compton	___ Lister
Jo. Fenwick	Hen. Pownall	Arth. Pargiter
Simon Needham	Tho. Best	___ Harecourt
Ben. Cicill	Jacob Stringer	John Gorge
Humph. Jones	___ Courtop	Tho. Roe
Jam. Gray	Ro. Harvie	Neale, Moses

Provost Marshall, John Yarner
Carriage-master, Caleb Love-joy
Chirurgion, Nath. Harris
Chaplain, William Sedgwick
Quarter-master, William Bradford

Colonel Ballards Regiment

Captaines	Lieutenants	Ensignes
Col. Tho. Ballard	Leon Moreton	Hen. Collingwood
Lieu. C. Fran. Martin	Jo. Hughes	William Fowles
Ser. Ma. Wil. Lower	Dan. Redman	Cha. Parker
Tho. Middleton	John Lookar	Robert Purpell
Fran. Foukes sen.	Fran. Fowke jun.	Henry Higgins
Edward Allen	Fran. Bowyler	Tho. Axstell
Edw. Primrose	Edw. Norbury	Jo. Hardy
Peter Momford	Robert Davies	Edw. Wett
Jo. Browne		William Ogee
Robert Noyes	Tho. Brandy	William Garfoot

Quarter-master, John Lamsdie
Waggon master, Jere. Burleigh
Provost Marshall, Ben. Ludlow

Sir William Fairfax his Regiment

Captaines	Lieutenants	Ensignes
C. Sir William Fairfax	David Goldsmith	John Read
L. Col. Will Monings	Thomas Whitney	Atwell Needham
Ser. Maj. Jarvis Paine	George Tirwhit	John Lloyd
Francis Rogers	John Caldecott	Richard Adams
Edward Ondingsell	William France	Richard Upton
Thomas Rush	Thomas Rutton	Edward Otter
Michael Bland	Francis Bland	James Sleigh
Robert Wilshiere	George Gifford	Jo. White
___ Leighton	William Llewellin	Theophilus Willey
William Trunke	John Foster	Samuel Kenarick

Quartermaster, Thomas Tyrer
Chirurgion, James Winter
Provost-Marshall, Henry Fisher
Carriage Master, Henry Ward

Colonell Charles Essex his Regiment

Captaines	Lieutenants	Ensignes
Coll. Charles Essex	Francis Hall	Jo: Shipman
L. C. Adam Coningham	Edward Barnewell	Leonard Hawkins
Ser. Maj. ___ ___	James Webb	Jo: Wheeler
William Roberts	Ralph Williams	Jo: Watkins
Jo: Jenkins	Barth. Elliot	Tracey Smart
Francis Hall	Walraven Hemert	Jo: Withers
William Frederick	Christoph. Crow	William Stratford
John Haselwood	Christoph. Chidley	Thomas Fitz

| Samuel Loftus | James Burrell | Robert Shergall |
| Sir William Essex | Daniel Robinson | Richard Thornehill |

Quartermaster, Roger Wase
Chaplain, Samuel Wells
Provost-Marshall, Martin Benthin
Chirurgion, Jo: Browne

Colonell John Hambden his Regiment

Captaines	*Lieutenants*	*Ensignes*
Coll. John Hambden	Henry Isham	Edward Willet
Lieu. C. ___ Wagstaff	A Dutchman	
Ser. Maj. Will. Barriff	___ Shorter	Laurence Almot
Richard Ingoldsbie		
___ Nicholls		
___ Arnett		
John Stiles		
___ Raymant		
Robert Farrington		
___ Morris		

Chaplaine, William Spurstow

How the number of Souldiers in each Regiment of Foot
are divided under their severall Captaines

The Colonells Company	200
The Lieutenant Collonells Company	160
The Serjeant Majors Company	140
Seven Captaines	700

Every Regiment consists of 1200 Besides Officers

The Names of the Counsell of War

Sir John Merick, President
Sir William Wardlaw
Colonell Grantham
Sir William Constable
Philbert Emmanuel de Boyse, Lieutenant General of the Artillery
Doctor Isaac Dorisla, Advocate of the Army

The List of the Troops of Horse, under the Command of William Earle of Bedford: Each Troop consisting of 60 horse, besides two Trumpeters, three Corporalls, a Sadler and a Farrier

Colonells and their Officers

Colonell, William Earle of Bedford
Major,
Chirurgion, Hugh Ward

Colonell, Sir William Balfore
Major, John Urrey
Chirurgion, James Swright [sic]

Colonell, Bazill Lord Fielding
Major, Robert Beckill
Chirurgion,

Colonell, Lord Willoughby of Parham
Major,
Chirurgion,

Collonell, Sir William Waller
Major, Horatio Carew
Chirurgion, James Bricknell

Colonell, Edwin Sands
Major, Alexander Douglas
Chirurgion, John Anthony

1. Troop
The L. Generals
Lieu. W. Ansell
Cornet, John Palmer
Quartermast.

2.
C. Sir William Balfore
L. John Meldram
C. William Jewty
Q.

3.
C. Lord Grey, Groub:
L. Sim. Matthewes
C. Tho. Barington
Q. David Madox

4.
C. Earl of Peterb.
L. Herb Dlausherd [sic]
C. Will. Cheney
Q.

5.
C. Lord Say
L. Henry Atkinson
C. John Croker
Q. Robert Parin

6.
C. Lord Brooke
L. Richard Crosse
C. Rob. Lilbourne
Q. John Okey

7.
C. Lord Hastings
L. Tho. Gratwick
C. Henry Aysluye
Q. Tho: Mesham

8.
C. Lord Saint John
L. Marmad. Couper
C. Oliver Cromwell
Q. Will. Wallen

9.
C. Lord Stanford
L. Samuell Bosa
C. Cap. Ri. Bingley
Q. Thomas Vaves

10.
C. Lord Fielding
L. Reeve Bayley
C. Tho. Brudnell
Q. William Tovey

11.
C. Lord Wharton
L. Ralph Whistler
C. Peter Ware
Q. Nich. Battersby

12.
C. L. Willoughby of P.
L. Hum. Brookbank
C. Tho. Hickman
Q.

13.[11]
C. Lord Grey
L.
C.
Q. ___ Madox

14.
C. James Sheffeld
L. Thomas Jewks
C. Rich: Maunder
Q. Richard Jolly

15.
C. Sir W: Waller
L. Ric: Newdigate
C. Foulke Grevill
Q. Francis Grey

16.
C. John Gunter
L. Henry Strelly
C. James Godderd
Q. Edw: Pudsey

17.[12]
C. William Pretty
L. Mat: Ploughman
C. Miles Morgan
Q. Nich: Smith

18.
C. Rob: Burrell
L. John Greene
C. Nathaniel West
Q. Thomas Eliot

---

[11] This appears to be a duplication of troop no. 3.
[12] Pretty's troop is duplicated, appearing also as no. 70, but with a different quartermaster.

19.
C. Francis Dowett
L. Hen: Sanderson
C. Thomas Gore
Q. John Otter

20.
C. James Temple
L. William Baker
C. Carax Ling
Q. Francis Sharpe

21.
C. John Bird
L. Samuell Bosa
C. Ambrose Rooke
Q. Jonathan Finch

22.
C. Mathew Draper
L.
C. John Strelly
Q. Abrah: Carter

23.
C. ___ Dimock
L.
C.
Q.

24.
C. Horatio Carey
L. Jonas Vandrusick
C. George Hutton
Q.

25.
C. John Alured
L.
C.
Q.

26.
C. John Neal
L. Rob: Bruse
C.
Q.

27.
C. John Hamond
L.
C. William Gill
Q. Isack Cavaler[13]

28.
C. Ed: Ayscough
L. Thomas Mosley
C. ___ Sayer
Q. ___ Clarke

29.
C. Alex: Pym
L. Arnold Haward
C. Rich: Compton
Q. Ralph Romitree

30.
C. John Hotham
L.
C.
Q.

31.
C. Arthur Evelin
L. C. Joh: de la Hay
C.
Q.

32.
C. Geo: Thompson
L. John Coyshe[14]
C. John Upton
Q. Will: Couse

---

[13] Name missing in the September version.
[14] 'Coshe' in the December version.

33.
C. Edwin Sandys
L. John Cockaine
C.
Q.

34.
C. Anth: Milemay
L. Hen: Hatcher
C. Sam: Cosworth
Q. Tho: Varnon

35.
C. Edw: Kyghley
L. Will: Cooker
C. Tho: Loftus
Q. Alex: Winchester

36.
C. Nath: Fines
L.
C.
Q.

37.
C. Edward Berry
L. C. Ed. Saunders
C. Tho: Billiard
Q. Hen: Woodnoth

38.
C. Alex. Douglas
L.
C.
Q.

39.
C. Tho. Lidcott
L. Robert Stradling
C.
Q.

40.
C. Tho. Hamond
L. John Lindsey
C. Mi: Wanderford
Q.

41.
C. John Dulbeir
L. Will: Framton
C. H: Vanbraham
Q. Jo. Downcham

42.
C. Francis Fines
L. James Moore
C. Henry Fines
Q. George Malten

43.
C. S. A. Haselwrick
L. Jervis Brakey
C. Tho: Horton
Q. Zach: Walker

44.
C. S. Walt: Earle
L. Ed. Johnson
C.
Q. Paul Scooler

45.
C. John Fleming
L. Robert Kirle
C. Ed: Fleming
Q. B. Blackborow

46.
C. Ar: Goodwin
L. John Browne
C. Peter Palmer
Q. William Jucey

47.
C. Rich: Grenvile
L. Charls Fountain
C. John James
Q. Alex: Davison

48.
C. Tho. Terrill
L. William Spry
C. Joseph Janes
Q. Ed: Throwley

49.
C. John Hale
L. Chenie Fuller
C. J. Midehoope
Q. Michael Hale

50.
C. H. Milmay of G.
L. Henry Gibb
C. Robert Milmay
Q. Edmund Hadon

51.
C. Will. Balfoore
L.
C. George West
Q.

52.
C. George Austin
L.
C.
Q.

53.
C. Adrian Scroope
L. William Day
C. Max: Vetty
Q. Henry Nuby

54.
C. Herc. Langrish
L. John Dingley
C. I. de la Blancheur
Q. John Ealsinan

55.
C. Edw. Wingate
L. Thomas Evans
C. Hen: Daldorne
Q. Jo: Whitbread

56.
C. Edw: Baynton
L.
C.
Q.

57.
C. Ch: Chichester
L. John Hide
C. Edward Weeks
Q. Richard Gourd

58.
C. Henry Ireton
L. John de Gennis
C. Samuel Clarke
Q. Christ: Briston

59.
C. Walter Long
L. Nich: Battersby
C. Coniers Cooper
Q. Walt: Harcourt

60.
C. John Fines
L. Jo: Carmichaell
C. Edw: Walley
Q. Will: Bugslock

61.
C. Fr: Thompson
L. Thomas Elliot
C. Vincent Corbet
Q. Phillip Barley

62.
C. Edmond West
L.
C.
Q.

63.
C. Sir Robert Pie
L.
C.
Q.

64.
C. Tho: Hatcher
L.
C.
Q.

65.
C. Robert Vivers
L.
C.
Q.

66.
C. Will: Anselme
L.
C.
Q.

67.
C. Oli: Cromwell
L. Cutbert Baildon
C. Jos. Waterhouse
Q. John Disbrow

68.
C. Robert Kirle
L. Ch: Fleming
C. James Kirle
Q. John Ball

69.
C. Sir Will: Wray
L.
C.
Q.

70.
C. William Pretty
L. Math: Plowman
C. Miles Morgan
Q. Anth: Arundell

71.
C. Sir Joh: Sanders
L. Will: Wardley
C. Matthew Pedar
Q. John Harding

72.
C. Tho: Temple
L.
C.
Q.

73.
C. Valen: Watton
L. Jarvis Bonner
C. ___ Watton
Q. Obadiah Crish

74.
C. Sir Faith: Fortescue
L.
C.
Q.

75.
C. Symon Rudgley
L. Lew: Chadwick
C. Edward Fines
Q.

Dragooners, Each Troope consisting of 100 Horse, Besides the Officers

1.
Colonell, and Capt: John Brown
Major and Cap: Nath: Gordon
Sir John Browne, Captaine

2.
Cap: Robert Mewer
Lieut: Thomas Mewer
Cor: Nicholas Mewer

3.
Cap: William Bucham
Cap: Robert Marine
Lieut: Francis Bradbury
Quartermaster, John Blackman
Provost-Marshall, Daniell Lyon

4.
Cap: Sir Anthony Irby
Lieut: William Patrick
Cor: Richard le Hunt

5.
Collonell: James Wardlo
Lieut: George Dunlas
Cap: Archibald Hambleton
Cap: Alexander Nerne
Cap: John Barne
Cap: James Stenchion
Chirurgion, James Heithley

Those Officers that are not mentioned in these Lists, have not as yet received their Commissions, by reason of their suddain imployment in the expedition.

[7]
A Copy of the List of all the Cavaliers of his Majesties Marching Army, with the number of Captaines, in each severall Regiment, and every Regiment containing about a thousand Souldiers.[15]

Printed Nov (Wing C6177); repr. 22nd Dec (TT E.64[4])

Imprimis I. Regiment
The Earle of Newcastle, Lord Generall of His Majesties foot Forces
Lieutenant Colonell Rich, Sergeant Major Babthorpe
Captaine Fleetwood, Captaine Waters, Captaine Hemings, Captaine Aston, Captaine Gyles, Captaine Fisher, Captaine Andrewes, Captaine Frost

2. Regiment
Colonell Lord Taffe an Irishman
Lieutenant Colonell Sir John Rodes, Sergeant Major Thomas Treveere
Captaine Upton, Captaine Hobbey, Captaine White, Captaine Hill, Captaine Farryer, Captaine Whiteacre, Captaine Floyd, Captaine Douglas, Captaine Winter

3. Regiment
Colonel Hastings
Lieutenant Colonel Langley, Sergeant Major Stanley
Captaine Fryer, Captaine Venner, Captaine Hodges, Captaine Johnson, Captaine Fisher

4. Regiment
Colonel Sir Thomas Glemham
Lieutenant Colonel Vaughan, Sergeant Major Wagstaffe
Captaine Long, Captaine Coney, Captaine Starkeley, Captaine Smart, Captaine Jackson

5. Regiment
Colonel Sir Francis Wortley
Lieutenant Colonel Russell, Sergeant Major Waller
Captaine Tukes, Captaine Stafford, Captaine Shelton

6. Regiment
Lord Grandison, Lieutenant Generall
Lieutenant Colonel John Digby, Sergeant Major Willoughby

---

[15] This list appears to have been culled from *A Most True Relation of the Present State of His Majesties Army...* (TT E.244[2]; list [7]), printed three weeks earlier on 3rd December.

Captaine Tempest, Captaine Morgan, Captaine Crane, Captaine Musgrave, Captaine Badger, Captaine Hillyard, Captaine Muggridge

7. Regiment
Colonel Endimion Porter
Lieutenant Colonel Vavasor, Sergeant Major Stanhope
Captaine Williams, Captaine Berry, Captaine Tisdale, Captaine White, Captaine Owen, Captaine Beesley, Captaine Thirlow

8. Regiment
Colonell Ashburnham
Lieutenant [Colonel] Bruerton, Sergeant Major Carey
Captaine Huet, Captaine Fowler, Captaine Ridgley, Captaine Washer, Captaine Bowen, Captaine Ballard, Captaine Weeks

9. Regiment fosborne
Colonell Bellasis
Lieutenant Colonell Murrey, Sergeant Major Pope
Captaine Holloway, Captaine Legge, Captaine Withers, Captaine Hodges, Captaine Homer, Captaine Metoo, Captaine Barret

10. Regiment
Viscount Kilmurrey, Sergeant Major Generall
Lieutenant Colonell Sir Faithfull Fortescue, Sergeant Major Pollard
Captaine Bulhead, Captaine Prowse, Captaine Thomas, Captaine Colesfoote, Captaine Atkinson, Captaine Bateman, Captaine Denby

11. Regiment
Sir Lewis Dives
Lieutenant Colonel Lucy, Sergeant Major Withrington
Captaine Browne, Captaine Thomas Furbush, Captaine Ley, Captaine Johnson, Captaine Slingsby

12. Regiment
Colonell Sir Charles Lucas
Lieutenant Colonell Stanley, Sergeant Major Kelley
Captaine Hodges, Captaine Ford, Captaine Burley, Captaine Strangewayes, Captaine Whiteaway

13. Regiment
Colonell Sir George Gotherick[16]
Lieutenant Colonell Washington, Sergeant Major Powell
Captaine Isaack, Captaine Johnson, Captaine Lever, Captaine Burrowes, Sutton

---

[16] An error: the colonel's first name was John. His surname was more usually 'Goodrick'.

14. Regiment
Colonell Osborne
Lieutenant Colonell Savage, Sergeant Major Oneale
Captaine Forster, Captaine Vaux, Captaine Holyday, Captaine Hussey, Captaine Buttler, Captaine Jones, Captaine Fidler

Prince Robert Generall of the Horse, Sir Thomas Byron chiefe Commander of the Princes Troope, containing about 500. Horse. The Earle of Bristoll two Troops. The Earle of Crawford three Troops. The Lord Digby, two Troops. Lord Capell, two Troops. The Lord Willoughby, two Troops. The Lord Grandison, Lord Killmurrey, Lord Rich, Sir Charles Lucas, Sir George Gothericke, Sir Francis Wortley, each of them a Troop of Horse; Besides a foot Regiment. Sir John Byron, one Troope of Horse.

I have omitted the Earle of Cumberland his Horse and foot, the Marquesse Hertfords Horse and foot, the Earle of Darbies Horse and foot, which is at the least, 16000.

None of which have been as yet with His Majestie, so that in all parts His Majesties Army of Horse and Foot is supposed to be 40000. Souldiers.

[8]
A most true relation of the present State of His Majesties Army

Printed 3rd Dec 1642, London (TT E.244[2]);[17]

A Most true relation of the present state of His Majesties Army; wherein also the truth of that declaration published by the Parliament, of their happy victory in the battaile at Keynton, is both justly asserted and abundantly proved, humbly presented by the author who was personally present, to the Honourable the Lords and Commons in Parliament assembled.

I Should thinke it a Sinne in mee beyond all Expiation, if I should not do my best, (and yet judge that too little) for preserving my own Country from that imminent Ruine, where with it is now threatned by his Majesties adverse Army, and not apprehending a more probable way thereto, then by nourishing love, and union in all of my own mynd, and, for that end, removing all these needles Panique fleares, whereunto the Common people are naturally too probe; I have here undertaken (for their further joy, and comfort,) both to shew them the condition of his Majesties present Army, and likewise the fortune of his former at Keynton upon which two Crutches (as not unfitt Supporters) their weakest Expectations may still with safety value. To say nothing of the matter, whereby it was atchieved, (which is better describ'd by the Parliaments Declaration, then it can be by my ruder, and more unpractized pen,) I will only insist of the matter of Victory, then obtained thereby the Parliament, though by the King denyed, which I prove by two reasons, that are equally unanswerable: first, because the King both lost more men, then the other side, and those of his, that fell, were a great deale more considerable, for the Quality of their Persons, and Dignity of their places; and secondly, in regard that their Army kept the Field, when the King's (upon its rowting) was gladd to steale away; I might rather say Flye, which they did with clypped wings: For no lesse, then five whole Regiments, (and those their very best, both for Number of men, and compleatnes of furniture) by name, **the Lord Generalls, Sir Raphe Duttone's, Colonell Blage's, Colonell Bollis's,** and **Sir Lewis Dyves**; which, though it scaped best, because he, and **Captain Slingsby** are yet left alive, all the other foure's Officers being wholly cutt of, together with the Souldiers that servd under their Command; yet that Regiment now hath nothing, but their bare lives to boast of: whereby it's heard condition is not rendered much better. I might likewise add a third as materiall for my purpose, and that is the new face of his Majesties present Army, dawb'd over with the Paynt of deluding Hypocrisy, wherein there is now few that commanded in the other, but new ones entertained, and many of them Papists, by name, the **Lord Viscount Taff**, Colonell of a Regiment of foot, with **Captain Thomas Trafford**, his Serjeant Major the **Lord Viscount Dillon**, captain of a troop of

[17] The original document is little more than a single chunk of unformatted text: for clarity, bold emphasis and paragraphing has been added by the present publisher. A number of typing errors have also been corrected.

Horse; **Captain Babthorp**, Serjeant Major to the **Earle of New-castle**, Colonell of a Regiment of foot, and the Kings new Generall of his whole Army; **Captain Stanley**, Serjeant Major to **Captain Henry Hastings**, now Colonell of a Regiment of foot, besides a thousand Dragoneeres, that he had before; **Captain Wagstaff**, Serjeant Major to **Sir Thomas Glentham**, Colonell of a Regiment of foot; **Captain John Digby**, younger sone to the Earle of Bristoll, Lieutenant Colonell to the **Lord Viscount Grandison's** Regiment of foot, who hath likewise another of Horse, and besides is Liutenant-Generall of his Majesties whole Army; master **Endymion Porter**, Colonell of a Regiment of foot; **Captain Murray**, Lieutenant Colonell to master **John Bellasis**, younger sone to the Lord Fauconbridg, and Colonell of a Regiment of Foot; another **Captain Stanley**, Lieutena[n]t Colonell to **Sir Charles Lucas**, Colonell of a Regiment of foot; **Captain Kelley**, an Irish man, Serjeant Major to the said Regiment; **Captain Roger Powell**, now prisoner here in Town, Serjeant Major to **Sir John Gooderick** Baronet, Colonell of a regiment of foot; and Captain of a troop of eight score Horse; **Captain Savage**, Lieutenant Colonell to **Sir Edward Osborne** Baronet, Colonell of a Regiment of foot; and **Captain Brien oneile**, Serjeant Major to the same; **Sir John Digby**, younger brother to Sir Kenelme, Captain of a troop of Horse; and one **master Stamford** of Warwickshire, his Cornett; **Sir John Smith**, Knight Banneret, (and so made, for recovering the Kings lost Standard,) Captain of a troop of Horse; **Sir John Beaumont**, Baronet, Colonell of another Regiment of foot; **Captain Dormer**, sone to master Anthony Dormer of Grovepark in Warwickshyr, one of Colonell Beaumonts private Captains, who hath many more of that Religion in his Regiment, though their names be unknown to me, and would willingly have no other, as this Relations Author by experience can affirme, who refused, for that reason, to be his eldest Captain, which command he did offer him at the graunt of his commission; and part of these Commanders left their charges in Ireland, (which suffers more in nothing, then in lack of able Leaders,) to receive imployment here from the King, as he pleaseth; by name **Sir Faithfull Fortescue** (most unworthy such a name) now Lieutenant Colonell to the Lord Viscount Killmorry, Colonell of a Regiment of foot, and Serjeant Major Generall of the Army; **Captain Roger Bradshagh**, Lieutenant Colonell to Captain Herbert Price Server to the Queene, who is Colonell of a regiment of foot; **Captain Henry Washington**, Lieutenant Colonell to Sir John Gooderick Baronet, Colonell of a Regiment of foot; **Captain Guy Moulsworth**, Lieutenant Colonell to the Lord Viscount Cromwell, Colonell of a Regiment of foot; **Captain Richard Willis**, (who had commission for a troop of horse in Ireland, but never came over,) Serjeant Major to the Lord Viscount Grandison's Regiment of Horse; **Captain Woodhouse**, that expected a Lieutenant Colonells place, but very lately had none; and **Captain Green**, (who had a commission for a company in Ireland, but never went over,) Serjeant Major to the Earle of Northampton's Regiment of foot[.]

[F]or the strength of the King's Army, it lye's chiefly in his Horse, whereof there are these Regiments, and no more, besides the Kings two troopes, the one of his own Servants, and some choice Volunteers, and the other of their Followers, both which are neere six hundred; First, **the Prince his own Regiment**, wherein are ten troopes; first his own, commanded by **Captain Thomas Byron**, who is likewise Serjeant Major of that Regiment; 2. **the Duke of Yorks**, first commanded by the **Lord d'Aubigny**, slayne in the battaile neare Keynton, and now by master **Charles Cavendish**, younger brother to the

Earl of Devonshire; 3. **Earle of Northamptons**; 4. the **Earle of Westmorlands**; 5. the **Earle of Crawfords**; 6. the **Lord Willoughbys** (now Earle of Lindsey) who hath likewise the command of the Kings life Guard; that consist's of two thousand, fifteen hundred whereof are footmen, and the rest Dragoneers; 7. **Sir Thomas d'Allisons**, a Lincolnshire Baronet, but a man of small meanes; though some way of great parts; 8. **Sir William Pennymans**, who hath likewise a regiment of foot, left behind at Bridgnorth by the Kings appointment, to secure his Subjects there, that opposed the Militia. 9. **Captain Thomas Sheltons**; 10. **Captain John Jacksons**, lately Gentlemen of the Horse to the Earle of Strafford.

The second Regiment of Horse belongs to **Prince Rupert**, which concists of seven troopes, but none of them half full; of their Captaines I know none, but **Captain Daniell Oneyle**, who, from being a Prisoner here, whence he strangely escaped, is mounted to the honour of Prince Ruperts Serjeant Major.

3. The **Earle of Carnarvans**, consisting of six troopes whose Serjeant Major is **Sir Charles Lucas**, now Colonell of a Regiment of foot besides;

4. The **Lord Viscount Grandisons**, consisting of six troopes, whose Serjeant Major is **Captain Richard Willis**;

Colonell Henry Wilmott's, consisting of six Troopes, who is Commissary-Generall of the Horse, and for his Sarjeant Major, hath **Captaine Edward Fielding**;

The sixth, and last of those, that are now with the King, is **Sir John Biron's**, who is Governour to the Duke of Yorke, and, for his Serjeant-Major hath his brother **Gilbert Biron**, wherein are but five Troopes, and those weakened much at Worcester:

Which is all his horse here, excepting Dragoneers, whereof there are these Regiments, and no more that I ever heard of.

1. **Colonell Hastings** his, that consists of a thousand, which indeed is a mixed Regiment, because halfe of them are Horse;

2. **Colonell Edward Greys**, younger brother to the Lord Grey of Werke, which consists of a thousand, but all Dragoneers;

3. **Colonell Gores**, younger brother to Sir Thomas Gore, high Sheriffe of Yorke-shire, which consists of a thousand, all Dragoneers likewise.

4. **Sir Edward Duncombes**, that consists of five hundred, whom the King hath made a Baronet, to his neighbours great envy, for the service, which hee did him in the view at Heyworth-more, where all the Yorkists mett to receave the Kings pleasure, which by Sir Edward Duncombe they were pressed to observe.

The last is that five hundred, which are part of the life Guard: and this, I am sure, is all his strength of Horse here, but what he hath elsewhere is to mee unknown. For his whole store of Ordinance, bee hath some thirty peeces, whereof eight are very large, some tenn of a middle, and the rest of smaller size for his store of Munition, it cannot bee much, because it is so sparingly given out to the Souldiers, whose small skill in Arithmatique can half number all the Cornes of it, (I meane of their powder) judge then what their Bullett is: and, for their store of Match, it may quickly bee O're matched. But, I think, as in the fury of his daring Cavalliers, to whom he is exhorted to give a firme Belieff, and a faithfull adherence, by the Clergy about him; with whom the Lawyers there doe Cooperate to that end; as men, that need the Ayde of their courage to protect them: amongst which the Lord Keeper, Sir Robert Heath, master Holborne, and master Hyde, are all that I know of. And, least the King should faile to remember what they say, they in the Church it selfe use the same Perswasions to him, choosing texts, for the purpose, so full of Ambiguity, as like the Delphique Oracle, will admitt a double sence; and God grant they delude not the best Christian King, as that did the foolish Pagans, that ranne thither for directions, how to manage their affaires, and appease their angry gods, who themselves were but dumbe idols, though the devill often spake in them.

Besides there are some Lords that are still about the King, of which the **Earles of Bristoll, Southampton**, and **Northampton**, with the **Lord Digby, Willoughby**, now in durance, **Falkland, Newark, Savile**, and **Dundsmore**, are the chiefe; and some other meaner Courtiers, all notorious Delinquents by name, Sir Edward Deering, and Sir George Beommon[?] Baronets, with Sir George Strode Knight, who are never unready to lend their best assistance, to make like impressions of hope in the King, that, for all his late defeate, he shall vanquish at the last: Whereby the pure Fountaine of His goodnesse being poysoned, such streames must needs run thence, as we see our Land o're-flowen with, even Rivers of bloud, and springs of griefe, and feare; and till those be dryed up by God's own Almighty hand, we can neither look for inward, nor so much, as outward peace: and our plenty in the interim being wholly consumed, we may all cry out, Ichabod, our glory is departed. But good Lord, of thy great mercy, so worke with our good King, in the opening of his eyes, and the softning of his heart, as to make him clearely see, by his speedy returne to us, or, whilst he staies from us, conscientiously to feele, that the depth of our sufferings, needs the height of his compassion: and that thence he may be brought to approve of this Maxime, that a King in nothing is, nor can be so happie, as in his peoples love, and his Kingdomes lasting peace.

But, to wrap up my sad story in a cheerefull Catastrophe, there are missing in this Army, which were Officers in the Battell, and therefore dead out-right, ill hurt, or taken Prisoners, by which means they are made useless for any further service, these that follow, with some more that I know not of. **Sir Ralph Dutton** himselfe, Colonell of a regiment foote, his Lieutenant-Colonell, **Captain Stephen Hawkings**; his Sarjeant Major, **Captaine Digory Collins**; Colonell Blage, his Lieutenant-Colonell, **Captaine George Lisle**, who had his Commission for a company in Ireland, but never came over; **Captaine Barnaby Scudamore**, Sarjeant Major to the same Regiment, **Colonell Bolles**, who was Sir John Clotworthyes Lieutenant Colonell there, **Cap. Richard Dewz**, brother to Sir Simonds Dewz, Lieutenant Colonell to Bolles, and **Cap. Nathaniel Moyle**, his Sarjeant Major, **Sir Thomas Danby** Lieutenant colonell to Mr John Bellasis, Colonell to a Regiment of foot, and **Cap. Immanuel Gilby**, Sarjeant Major to the same; The Lord Generall's Lieutenant-Colonell, **Captain Mountros, Cap Thomas Sherley**, Lieutenant-Colonell to Sir Lewis Dives regiments, & **Captaine Gervase Holles**, Sarjeant Major to the same.

At length my work is finished, which went on much the stronger through my willingnesse to leave nothing that was needful unmentioned: which now done, instead of proving me the Father of a Lye, will rather prove Truth to bee the Daughter of Time. *Utilitatis servus publica, sicut vestra Amplitudinis, ignotarum ignotisimus.*

My Lords, and Gentlemen,

Touching your first proposition, which was for my acquainting you with the names of those other Commanders, whereof I made no mention, that are absent this time from His Majesties Army, by the ___ of present sicknesse, late death, or forc'd restraint, my Answer is this, which I wish you to confide in. **Our Lord Generall** then shot, is since dead of his hurts; **Sir Edmond Verney**, His Majesties then Knight-Marshall, and Standard-bearer, fell dead in the field; **Captaine Robert Townes-end**, one of the Lord Generalls private captaines, and **Captaine Bellingham**, who (as I take it) was of Colonell Bellasis his Regiment, with **Sir Henry Reeve**, His Majesties eldest Pentioner dyed, and were buryed all three at Oxford,[18] whence **Sir Gilbert Gerard**, (farre-Country Captaine) but now Lieutenant Colonell to the Lord-Viscount Molyneux his Regiment, (who here is called, and generally believed to be Ballard, as Sarjeant Major Willis is likewise nick-named Wallis, for so I finde them mentioned in some published false papers,) was carryed at that time very sicke to the Country, where since (as we heare) hee is dead of his wounds. There were taken in the or on the way, I meane betwixt Keynton, and Oxford) these which follow, the then Lord Willoughby, but now **Earle of Lindsey, Sir Edward Stradling** Baronett, Colonell of a Regiment of foote, **Sir Henry Radley** a Lincolnshyre Knight, and one of the private Captaines of the Lord Generalls Regiment, **Sir Thomas Lunsford** Colonell of a foote Regiment, and come lately to the King from the westerne Army; Sir Gilbert Gerard before mentioned; **Colonell William Vavsor** now, but Lieutenant-Colonell under the said Lord Willoughby of His Majesties Life-guard whose brave Sarjeant Major **Captaine William Leighton**, lost in the battaile is since much lamented; **Sarjeant-Major Willis**, who serves under the Lord Grandison in his regiment of Horse; master **James Strange-wayes**, Coronet to Sir Lewis Dyve his brother in lawes troopes, one **Master White a lieutenant**, but to whom I know not; with very many more, whose names I never heard of, touching the number of common souldiers lost, I am sure when our Army came next to be reviewed, we lacked of kill'd, and run-awayes, three thousand at leasy; which shall be my answer to that Proposition.

For the third, touching His Majesties behaviour of himselfe upon the march, I must thereto reply, if I shall deale ingeniously, he disarm'd the Trayned-bands every where, as he past, a Strategem devised, and Traine layd for that purpose, which was this; the very day before he marched away from Nottingham, (for till then, but a few of our Souldiers were halfe-armed, for which cause they ner'e but once there were viewed in a full body, hee sent to the High Sheriffe of Derbishire, to wait on him the next day, with the Trained Bands at Derby, (as before hee had done to the other of Nottinghamshire) and they met him accordingly in their compleate proper Armes, where still after he had tooke up his lodging, he gave order, that foure, or five Drummes should beat up and down the Towne, commanding the Trained souldiers to bring in all their Armes, (and that I must needs say, upon paine of death,) either to the Town-Hall or some other such place, where there still were some appointed to receave them for His use and the Sarjeant Major Generall for the most part was then present: and thus the most were got, but yet some by meere force, the Cavaleers still taking them where they chanced to find them, not without the

---

[18] Townsend on 7th November at St Mary Magdalen; Reeves on the 8th at All Saints, and Henry Bellingham on 13th at St Mary the Virgin (S.F. Jones (ed.), *Royalist Burials at Oxford 1642-1651*, 2015).

Kings approvement, though perhaps without his privity: And, as for His provision of Victuall for Himselfe or carriage, for His Ordnance, or Baggage, they were brought in by the Country upon His speciall warrant (all Refusors to contribute being layd by the heeles) but yet paid for (as I heard) at his Majesties easie rates; for the fourth, which was the cause why I did desert His Army, (as I may seeme to doe, by my so departing from it) in answer thereunto, I must alledge these Motives.

First, I neither could get pay, not knew how to live without it, and,

Secondly, (to speake Truth) it was not my least Trouble, to see Papists swarme so in His Majesties Army, and receave that countenance from him, as to bee made his Colonels; against whose religion he had so much protested, for their more than Jewish cruelty, and worse than Turkish villany, to the poore Irish Protestants, whom they have so long afflicted, for the last, which was the number of the Irish runna-gates, that still follow His Army upon all removalls, I way averr the boldlyer, because I oft had seene it, of men, women, and Children, there is still at least t hree hundred; all waiting for imployment in any gainefull way: which made me (though no Coward) feare to march amongst them. Thus I have in much weaknesse exprest my greater willingnesse, both to your just commands, and to serve my deare Country.

[9]
A Catalogue of the Names of the Dukes, Marquesses, Earles and Lords, that have Absented themselves from the Parliament, and are now with His Majestie

Printed 22nd Dec, London (TT E.64[4])

The Lord Keeper; The Duke of Richmond
Marquesse of Hertford; Marquesse Hamilton
Earle of Cumberland
Earle of Bathe
Earle of Southampton
Earle of Dorset
Earle of Salisbury
Earle of Northampton
Earle of Devonshire
Earle of Carlile
Earl of Clare
Earle of Westmorland
Earle of Monmouth
Earle of Lindsey
Earle of Newcastle
Earle of Dover
Earle of Carnarvan
Earle of Newport
Earle of Thanet
Lord Moubray
Lord Strange
Lord Willoughby
Lord Longavill
Lord Rich
Lord Andover
Lord Faulckonbridge
Lord Lovelace
Lord Paulet
Lord Newarke
Lord Coventry
Lord Savill
Lord Dunsmore
Lord Seymour
Lord Capell

[10]
A List of his Majesties Navie Royall, and Merchants Ships... [Apr 1643]

Printed 22nd Apr 1643, London (Wing L2393)

His Majesties Ships
1. *Prince Royall,* Robert Earle of Warwick Admirall, Richard Blyth Capt., 500 men, 70 ordnance.
2. *St. Andrew*, William Batten Capt. Vice Admirall, 260 men, 45 ordnance.
3. *St. George*, Richard Owen Capt. Rere-Admirall, 260 men, 46 ordinance.
4. *Swift-sure*, Robert Moulton, Capt. 260 men, 48 ordinance.
5. *James,* H. Bethell, Capt. 260 men, 50 ordnance.
6. *Raine-bow*, Peter Andrewes, Capt. 240 men, 42 ordnance.
7. *Victory*, Nathanael Goodlad, Capt. 260 men, 46 ordnance.
8. *Charles*, Trestram Stevens of Dover Capt. 350 men, 46 ordnance.
9. *Converteine*, John Stanesby, Capt. 200 men, 42 ordnance.
10. *Anthelop*, ___ Haddock, Capt. 160 men, 36 ordnance.
11. *Entrance*, J. Bowen, Capt. 160 men, 40 ordnance.
12. *Leopard*, Ben. Cranley Capt. 160 men, 44 ordnance.
13. *Swallow*, Thom. Rainborow Capt. 150 men, 34 ordnance.
14. *Dreadnought*, ___ Soamaster, Capt. 140 men, 40 ordnance.
15. *Mary Rose*, Rich. Blyth jun. Capt. 100 men, 38 ordnance.
16. *8 Whelp*, Will. Thomas, Capt. 60 men, 18 ordnance.
17. *10 Whelp*, R. Hill, Capt. 60 men, 14 ordinance.
18. *Greyhound*, Abraham Wheeler, Capt. 50 men, 18 ordnance.
19. *Nichodemus*, J. Wood Com. & Master, 45 men, 10 ordnance.
20. *Hart*, ___ Batts Co. & Mr. 40 men, 12 ordnance.
21. *Hinde*, Robert Bramble, Com. and Mr. 70 men, 10 ordnance.
22. *Fortune* Pynk, Rich. Billard Com. and Mr. 14 men, 8 ordnance.

These two small Vessels, and the foure Ketches are to attend the Fleet.
23. *Nottordam*, Peter White Com. & Master, 20 men, 6 ordnance.
24. *Revenge*, J. Mildmay C. & Mr. 12 men, 4 ordnance.
25. *Prosperous*, Rich. Thompson Master.
26. *Anne*, Math. Berry Master.
27. *Hopewell*, Christopher Berry Master.
28. Loads boat at Dover.

Merchants Ships
1. *Martin*, Geo. Martin Capt. 532 tonne, 359 men, 36 ordnance.
2. *Hopefull Luke*, Robert Lea, Capt. 355 tonne, 106 men, 26 ordnance.
3. *Maydenhead*, James Lutton, Capt. 285 tonne, 85 men, 20 ordnance.
4. *Anne and Joyce*, Thomas Joans, Capt. 300 tonne, 90 men, 22 ordnance.
5. *Hercules*, Lawrence Moyer, Capt. 468 tonne, 135 men, 28 ordnance.
6. *Mayflower*, Jo. Piggot, Capt. 405 tonne, 121 men, 28 ordnance.
7. *Scipio*, Tho. Evane, Capt. 425 tonne, 127 men, 28 ordnance.
8. *Leopard*, Tho. Clark, Capt. 362 tonne, 108 men, 22 ordnance.
9. *Friendship*, Jo. Blake, Capt. 366 tonne, 109 men, 24 ordnance.
10. *Speedwell*, Ben. Peters, Capt. 383 tonne, 115 men, 26 ordnance.
11. *Providence*, Wil. Swanley, Capt. 270 tonne, 81 men, 20 ordnance.
12. *John and Barbary*, Jo. Barker Capt. 283 tonne, 84 men, 20 ordnance.
13. *Golden Lion of Leech*, Lodwick Dick, Capt. 450 tonne, 135 men, 30 ordnance.
14. *Exchange*, John Rochester, Capt. 326 tonne, 97 men, 24 ordnance.
15. *Golden Angel*, Richard Lucas, Capt. 341 tonne, 102 men, 26 ordance.
16. *Blessing*, Tho. Shaftoe, Capt. 200 tonne, 60 men, 18 ordnance.
17. *Prosperous*, Wil. Driver, Capt. 435 tonne, 130 men, 28 ordnance.
18. *Elizabeth and Anne*, Wil. Coppin, Capt. 88 tonne, 28 men, 18 ordnance.
19. *Blessing*, ___ Ashmore, Capt. 350 tonne, 105 men, 26 ordnance.
20. *George of Dover*, Geo. Bowden, Capt. 121 tonne, 36 men, 12 ordnance.
21. *James Youghall*, Tho. Morgan, Capt. 100 tonne, 40 men, 8 ordnance.
22. *Charity*, Ralph Dansk, Capt. 120 tonne, 36 men, 6 ordnance.
23. *Joslyn*, ___ Stansby, Capt. 196 tonne, 59 men, 12 ordnance.

Colliers Ships
Recovery, John North Command. 360 tonne, 70 men, 11 ordnance.
Edward and Elizabeth, Edw. Leigh Com. 350 tonne, 80 men, 14 ordnance.
Dragon, Jam. Peacocke Com. 260 tonne, 60 men, 6 ordnance.
Hector, Jam. Beddall Com. 360 tonne, 70 men, 20 ordnance.

Fire Ships
Swan, Rob. Hudson, Com. 200 tonne, 12 men.
Sarah, Lambert Pitches, Com. 250 tonne, 14 men.
Andrew and John, Thom. Craft, Com. 220 tonne, 13 men.
Lyon of London, James Flawes, Com. 220 tonne, 12 men.

His Majesties Ships for the Irish Coasts
1. *Bonadventure*, Richard Swanley Capt. Admirall, 170 men, 36 ordnance.
2. *Lyon*, Wil. Smith Cap. Vice Admirall, 170 men, 42 ordnance.
3. *Expedition*, Joseph Jorden Capt. Rere Admirall, 100 men, 15 ordnance.
4. *Providence*, William Brook Captaine, 100 men, 16 ordnance.
5. *Cressent*, Tho. Pluncket Com. & Mr. 50 men, 10 ordnance.
6. *Lilly*, John Lambert Com. & Mr. 60 men, 12 ordnance.

7. *Starre*, Tho. Cook Com. & Mr. 60 men, 12 ordnance.
8. *Signet*, J. Weild Co. & Mr. 70 men, 10 ordnance.

Merchants Ships
1. *Employment*, Tho. Ashley, Capt. 440 tonne, 132 men, 30 ordnance.
2. *Ruth*, Robert Constable, Capt. 400 tonne, 120 men, 24 ordnance.
3. *Peter*, Peter Strong, Capt. 170 tonne, 81 men, 14 ordnance.

Ten Merchant ships on the coast of Ireland, to be paid the freight, victuall, and wages unto the Owners and company, out of such moneys as have been or shall be paid in by the Adventurers upon the Act of subscription for Ireland, within one year after the date of the Order.

1. *Zant Merchant*, 390 tonne, 117 men.
2. *Good Hope*, 390 tonne, 117 men.
3. *Achilles*, 260 tonne, 78 men.
4. *Geo. Bonad.*, 242 tonne, 72 men.
5. *Mary Bonad.*, 240 tonne, 72 men.
6. *Hopewell*, 220 tonne, 66 men.
7. *Katherine*, 200 tonne, 60 men.
8. *Pennington*, 135 tonne, 40 men.
9. *Dolphin*, 100 tonne, 30 men.
10. *Peter*, 150 tonne, 45 men.

It is Ordained by the Lords and Commons in Parliament, That there should be allowed ten shillings per man, rigging, wages unto the Merchant Ships, and 19 shillings per Moneth a man, to all common Sea-men, when they are at Sea. And it is further ordered, for the better enouragement of the Officers and Sea-men, who shal be employed in the Fleet; there shall bee allowed unto those in the Kings Ships, besides their pay, one full third part of all Prizes that they shall take in this their employment: The other two thirds to bee reserved to the State, and to those in the Merchant Ships, one full third part for the Officers and Sea-men, and another third part to the Owners, and the third part reserved to the State as aforesaid; which divisions are to bee according to the custom of men of warre.

Bibliography

Brydges, Sir Egerton. *Collins's Peerage of England; Genealogical, Biographical, and Historical.* Nine vols. London: F. C. and J. Rivington and others, 1812.

Jones, S. F. (ed.). *Royalist Burials at Oxford 1642-51.* London: Tyger's Head Books, 2015. Limited edition publisher's pamphlet; collated from Oxford parish registers.

Peacock, Edward (ed.). *The Army Lists of the Roundheads and Cavaliers, Containing the Names of the Officers in the Royal and Parliamentary Armies of 1642.* Second edition. London: Chatto & Windus, 1874.

Rushworth, John. *Historical Collections. The Second Part, Containing the Principal Matters Which happened from the Dissolution of the Parliament, On the 10th of March, 4. Car. I. 1628/9. Until the Summoning of another Parliament, which met at Westminster, April 13. 1640.* London: 1686.

Calendar of State Papers, Domestic Series, of the Reign of Charles I. 1640. Preserved in Her Majesty's Public Record Office. Hamilton, William Douglas (ed.). London: Longmans & Co., 1880.

Calendar of State Papers, Domestic Series, of the Reign of Charles I. 1640-41. Preserved in Her Majesty's Public Record Office. Hamilton, William Douglas (ed.). London: Longmans & Co., 1882.

Mercurius Aulicus. Communicating the intelligence, and affairs of the Court, to the rest of the Kingdome. The first Weeke. 1st-7th January 1643. London, 1643.

The Army and Navy Lists – full details

[1] *List of the Strength of the Kings Majesties Army, both Officers and Soldiers, as they they were Mustered* [Rushworth, first list].

[1] *The Names of all the Collonels, Lieutenant Collonels, Sergeant Majors, Captains, Lieutenants,Ensignes, Preachers, Chirurgeons, Quarter Masters, Provost Marshals under his Excellency the Earl of Northumberland, Captain General for this Expedition 1640. Taken according to the Muster Roll after the Armies Retreat from Newcastle into Yorkshire* [Rushworth, second list].

[1] *A list of the Colonels as also of the severall Counties out of which they are to raise their Men, as also the Names of Ships, Captaines, and Lieutenants that are now set forth under the Command of the Right Honourable Algernoun Percey the Earle of Northumberland &c. Generall and Admirall of his Majesties Armie and Fleete for this this Expedition, 1640.* London? 1640. One page, STC 19616.

[2] *A List of the Field-Officers chosen and appointed for the Irish Expedition, by the Committee at Guild-hall London, for the Regiments of 5000. foot and 500. horse, Under the command of Philip Lord Wharton, Baron of Scarborough, Lord Generall for Ireland.* London: 11th June 1642. One page, BL 669.f.6(31). Reprinted December 1642, in TT E.64[4].

[3] *A List of the Names of Such Persons Who are thought fit for their Accommodation, and the furtherance of the Service in Ireland, to be entertained as Reformadoes; And to receive the halfe Pay due to the severall Officers here under named, untill opportunity be offered, according to their merit, further to prefer them; or that Order be given to the contrary, by the Committee at Guildehall London, 1642.* London: 16th June 1642. One page, BL 669.f.6(32).

[4] *A List of his Majesties Navie Royall, and Merchants Ships, their Names, Captains, and Lieutenants, their Men and Burthens in every one, now setting forth for the Guard of the narrow Seas, and for Ireland this yeare 1642.* Included in TT E.64[4], printed December 1642. This list, like several others in E.64[4], was probably a reprint of an earlier one.

[5] *A Catalogue of the Names of the Lords that subscribed to Levie Horse to assist His Majestie in defence of His Royall Person, the Two Houses of Parliament, and the Protestant Religion.* Dated June 1642, at York; printed July, at London. Wing N1033. Reprinted December 1642, in TT E.64[4].

[6] *The List Of The Army Raised under the command of his Excellency, Robert Earle of Essex and Ewe, Viscount Hereford, Lord Ferrers of Chartley, Bourcheir and Lovaine: Apponted Captaine Generall of the Army, Imployed for the defence of the Protestant Religion, the safety of his Majesties Person, and of the Parliament; the preservation of the Lawes, Liberties, and Peace of the Kingdom, and protection of his Majesties Subjects from violence and oppression. With the Names of the several Officers belonging to the Army.* London: September 1642. TT E.117[3]. Reprinted December 1642, in TT E.64[4].

[7] *A Copy of the List of all the Cavaliers of his Majesties Marching Army, with the number of Captaines, in each severall Regiment, and every Regiment containing about a thousand Soldiers.* London: November 1642. One page, Wing C6177. Reprinted December 1642, in TT E.64[4].

[8] *A Most True Relation of the Present State of His Majesties Army; Wherein also the truth of that Declaration published by the Parliament, of their happy Victory in the Battaile at Keynton, is both justly asserted and abundantly proved, humbly presented by the Author who was personally present, to the Honourable the Lords and Commons in Parliament assembled.* London: 3rd December, 1642. TT E.244[2].

Bibliography

[9] *A Catalogue of the Names of the Dukes, Marquesses, Earles and Lords, that have Absented themselves from the Parliament, and are now with His Majestie.* London: December 1642. TT E.64[4].

[10] *A List of his Majesties Navie Royall, and Merchants Ships, their Names, Captains, Men, Ordnance, in every Ship, now set forth for the Guard of the narrow Seas, and for the Coast of Ireland in this present expedition, 1643. Under the command of the Right Honourable Robert Earle of Warwick, Admirall and Commander in Chiefe of the said Fleet.* London, April 1643. One page, Wing L2393.

Index

- Entries marked with a star * should be treated with caution as they derive from lists [7] and [8], which are of dubious accuracy.
- Names in [square brackets] are known from other sources

Abdy, Sir Christopher, 14
Adama, Thomas, 32
Adams, Richard, 45
Adney, Clodius, 20
Albany, Thomas, 40
Alcorne (or Alcaron), Dr. Edward, 15
Aldridge (or Aldrich), Edward, Maj. F. under Sir Nicholas Byron 1640, 19; Lieut. Col. F. reformado 1642, 29; Lieut. Col. F. under Lord Rochford Sep 1642, 41
Alford, William, 12
Allanby, Thomas, 24
Allen, Edward, Capt. F. under Thomas Ballard Jun 1642, 25; same, Sep 1642, 45
Allen, John, 23
Allen, Thomas, 23
Allenson (or Allanson), Christopher, Quart. to William Bamfield's regiment, Jun 1642, 32; same, Sep 1642, 44
Alured, John, 49
Alured, Launce, 43
Anderson, Antony, 29
Anderson, James, 30
Andover, Charles Howard, Viscount, 'Lord Andover', subscription to levy horse for the King, Jun 1642, 36; confirmed as having sided with the King Dec 1642, 65
Andrew, ___, Lieut. of merchant ship *Samson* Dec 1642, 34
Andrewes, ___, Capt. F. under Earl of Newcastle Nov 1642, 55*
Andrewes, ___, Lieut. F. under Sir Henry Cholmley Sep 1642, 43
Andrewes (or Andrews), Edward, Capt. F. under Sir William Ogle 1640, 18; Maj. F. under Lord St. John 1642, 41
Andrewes, Thomas, Lieut. F. under Sir John Dougless 1640, 20
Andrewes, William, Ens. F. under Sir William Ogle 1640, 18
Andrews, Andrew, Quart. H. reformado Jun 1642, 29
Andrews, John, Lieut. under Sir James Hamilton 1640, 20
Andrews, Peter, Capt. of merchant ship *Mary Flower* Dec 1642, 34; navy, Capt. of *Rainbow* Apr 1643, 67
Ansell, William, 47
Anselme, William, Lieut. H. reformado Jun 1642, 29; Capt. H. Sep 1642, 52
Anthony, John, 47
Apew, John, Ens. F. under Earl of Peterborough 1642, 39. Probably 'Ap Hugh', or

'Pugh'. There is also an Ens. 'John Pew' listed in the regiment, suggesting a list error or printing mistake.
Apleby, Thomas, 43
Apleyard, [Matthew], 16
Appleton (or Apleton), Robert, Capt. F. under Richard Feilding 1640, 13, 21
Apseley, Edward, 44
Armory, Edward, 10
Arnett, ___, 46
Arundell, Anthony, Quart. H. under William Pretty Sep 1642, 52. Pretty's troop is duplicated in the list: in the other instance, a different officer appears as quartermaster.
Ascough – *see also* Ayscough
Ascough, Robert, 21
Ash, Simon, 42
Ashcough, Cecil, 23
Ashburnham, William, Lieut. Col. F. under Earl of Northumberland 1640, 9; Col. F. Nov 1642, 56*
Ashfield, Jo., Ens. F. to Henry Shelley under Lord Kerry Jun 1642, 25; Lieut. F. under Lord Brooke Sep 1642, 41
Ashley, Henry, Capt. F. reformado Jun 1642, 29; Capt. F. under Thomas Grantham Sep 1642, 44
Ashley, James, 30
Ashley, Thomas, Capt. of merchant ship *Employment* Apr 1643, 69
Ashly, ___, 34
Ashmore, ___, Capt. of merchant ship *Blessing* Apr 1643, 68
Ashton, Miles, 41
Asly, Thomas, 34
Atkinson, ___, 56*
Astley (or Ashley), Bernard, 10
Astley (or Ashley), Edward, 10
Astley (or Ashley), Sir Jacob, 10
Aston, ___, Capt. F. under Earl of Newcastle Nov 1642, 55*
Aston, Arthur, Col. F. 1640, 13
Aston, Francis, Ens. F. under Arthur Aston 1640, 13
Atchason, James, 40
Atkins, John, 13
Atkins, Jonathan, 9
Atkins, William, 17
Atkinson, Henry, 48
Auberry, ___, 15
d'Aubigny, George Stewart 9th Seigneur d'Aubigny, commanded Duke of York's regiment of horse but k. Edgehill; Dec 1642, 61*
Audey, Thomas, 17
Austin, George, 51
Austin, John, 11

Axtell, Thomas, 45
Ayleworth (or Ailworth), Walter, Capt. F. reformado Jun 1642, 29; Maj. F. under Lord Brooke Sep 1642, 41
Ayres, Thomas, 38
Ayscough – *see also* Ascough
Ayscough, Ed., 49
Aysluye, Henry, 48
Babthorpe, ___, Maj. F. under Earl of Newcastle Nov 1642, 55*; Dec 1642, 58*
Bacon, Robert, 18
Badger, ___, 56*
Baggett, Henry, 17
Bagot, Richard, 24
Baildon, Cutbert, 52
Baily – *see also* Bayley
Baily, Christopher, 40
Baily, John, Capt. F. under Sir John Merrick Sep 1642, 39
Bainfield, Jo., 26
Baker, James, 40
Baker, Robert, Capt. F. under William Bamfield Jun 1642, 26; Capt. F. under same Sep 1642, 43
Baker, William, Cor. H. reformado Jun 1642, 29; Lieut. H. under James Temple Sep 1642, 49
Baldwin (or Baldwine), John, Provost Marshall to Lord Barrymore 1640, 13; Provost Marshall General 1642, 37
Balfore (or Belfoore), Sir William, Lieut. Gen. H. & Col. H. Sep 1642, 37, 47, 51
Ball, Andrew, 44
Ball, John, 52
Ballard, ___, Capt. F. under William Ashburnham Nov 1642, 56*
Ballard, Benjamin, Corp. H. under Alexander Nayrne Jun 142, 23
Ballard, Francis, Lieut. F. under Lord Mandeville Sep 1642, 42
Ballard, Phillip, Lieut. F. under Lord Grandison 1640, 12; Capt. F. under Lord Rochford 1642, 41
Ballard, Thomas, Lieut. Col. F. under Lord Grandison 1640, 12; Col. F. Jun 1642 25, 31; Sep 1642, 45
Balston (or Balstone), John, Lieut. F. reformado Jun 1642, 30; Lieut. F. under Earl of Peterborough Sep 1642, 39
Balyes, William, 20
Bamfeild (or Bamfield), Joseph, Lieut. to Henry Wentworth 1640, 14; Maj. to Earl of Essex 1642, 38
Bamfield, William, Col. F. Jun 1642, 26; Sep 1642, 43
Banard, ___, 18
Bancks, Thomas, 20
Bankes, Sir John, 36
Barbar, Robert, 38
Barber, Thomas, 24

Barbridge, John, 11
Barington, Thomas, 47
Barke, William, 43
Barker, Francis, 44
Barker, Henry, 18
Barker, Jo., Capt. of merchant ship *John and Barbary* Apr 1643, 68
Barker, Robert, 21
Barley, Phillip, 52
Barne, John, 53
Barnet, Nicholas, 20
Barns, Bartholomew, 30
Barnes, Thomas, 40
Barnwell (or Barnewell), Edward, Lieut. F. under Charles Essex Jun 1642, 26; same, Sep 1642, 45
Baron, Richard, 42
Barrell, James, 26
Barret, ___, 56*
Barriff, William, 46
Barriffe, Thomas, 25
Barry, David, Lieut. F. under Earl of Barrymore, 12
Barry, Garret, 12
Barry, John, 13
Barry, Nicholas, 13
Barry, Phillip, 13
Barry, Richard, 13
Barry, William, 13
Barrymore (or Barramore), 1st Earl of (David Barry), 12
Barsey, James, 20
Barwick, Daniell, 38
Bascarvell, ___, Capt. F. under Sir Charles Vavasour 1640, 16
Bascarvell, Thomas, Lieut. F. under Sir Charles Vavasour 1640, 16
Baskavell, ___, Capt. F. under William Vavasour 1640, 17
Baskervill, Giles, 20
Basset, ___, Maj. F. under Sir William Ogle 1640, 18
Basset, Arthur, Maj. F. under Sir John Dougless 1640, 20
Basset, Buffy (Bussy?), 40
Bassett, James, Lieut. F. under Sir Thomas Glemham 1640, 14
Bateler, William, 43
Bateman, ___, 56*
Bath, Henry Bourchier 5th Earl of, subscription to levy horse for the King, Jun 1642, 35; confirmed as having sided with the King Dec 1642, 65
Batten, William, navy, *Saint George* Dec 1642, 33; Capt. of *St. Andrew* Apr 1643, 67
Batters, William, Col. Capt. reformado 1642, 30
Batters, William, Gentleman of the Ordnance 1642, 31
Battersby, Nicholas, Quart. H. under Lord Wharton Jun 1642, 23; same, Sep

1642, 48
Battersby, Nicholas, Lieut. H. under Walter Long Sep 1642, 51
Batts, ___, navy, Commander & Master of *Hart* Apr 1643, 67
Baxter, Salathiel, 21
Bayles, Robert, 20
Bayley – *see also* Baily
Bayley, John, Capt. F. under Francis Hamond 1640, 21
Bayley, Jo., Capt. F. reformado Jun 1642, 29
Bayley, Reeve, Lieut. H. under Lord Feilding, 48
Baynard, Adam, Lieut. H. to John Trenchard, Jun 1642, 24; Lieut. carbines to Sir Philip Stapleton under Earl of Essex, Sep 1642, 39
Baynton, Edward, 51
Baynton, James, 10
Beamont, John, 14
Beare, William, 21
Beaumont, Sir John, Maj. F. under Sir Thomas Glemham 1640, 14; Col. F., mentioned Dec 1642, 60*
Beckill, Robert, 47
Beddall, James, Commander of collier ship *Hector* Apr 1643, 68
Bedealls, Thomas, 41
Bedford, William Russell 5th Earl of, Lord General of H. and Col. of H. Sep 1642, 37, 47
Bedingfeild, William, 17
Bedolph, Michael, 11
Beecher, Henry, 44
Beecher, Lionell, Ens. under Sir Thomas Culpepper 1640, 16; Waggon Master to Colonel Bamfield's Regiment 1642, 32
Beecher, Oliver, 41
Beesley, ___, 56*
Beeston, Hugh, 42
Bellamy, William, 21
Bellasis (usu. Belasyse), [John], Col. F. Nov 1642, 56*; Dec 1642, 60*; list [8] reports Lieut. Col. as dead, hurt or captured, 62*
Bellasis (or Bellowes), William, Capt. F. under Sir Jacob Astley 1640, 11
Bellow, William, 17
Benbricke, Robert, 20
Bendish, Roger, 21
Bennet, ___, Capt. F. under Denzell Hollis Sep 1642, 43
Bennet, John, Ens. F. under Lord Grandison 1640, 12
Bennet, Robert, Corp. H. under Lord Brogill Jun 1642, 23
Bennett, ___, Chirurgion to Sir Charles Vavasour's regiment 1640, 16
Bennett, Henry, Capt. Ens. F. reformado 1642, 30
Bennett, Thomas, Lieut. F. under Sir William Ogle 1640, 18
Benson, Richard, Capt. firelocks under William Bamfield Jun 1642, 27; Capt. F. under same Sep 1642, 43

Benthin, Martin, 46
Berkshire, Thomas Howard 1st Earl of, 36
Berry, ___, Capt. F. under Endimion Porter Nov 1642, 56*
Berry, Christopher, navy, Master of ketch *Hopewell*, attendant on the fleet, Apr 1643, 67
Berry, Edward, Capt. H. Sep 1642, 50
Berry, John, Maj. F. under Marquess of Hamilton 1640, 18
Berry, Math., navy, Master of ketch *Anne*, attendant on the fleet, Apr 1643, 67
Berry, Samuell, Gentleman of the Ordnance Sep 1642, 38
Best, Thomas, Ens. F. under Marquess of Hamilton 1640, 19
Best, Thomas, Lieut. F. under Sir William Constable Sep 1642, 44
Bethell, H__, navy, Capt. of *James* Apr 1643, 67
Betsworth, Benjamin, 44
Bettridge, Roger, 38
Betts, George, 15
Bifield, Adoniram, 43
Billard, Richard, navy, Commander & Master of pynk *Fortune* Apr 1643, 67
Billiard, Thomas, 50
Billingsley, Henry, Col. F. reformado Jun 1642, 29; Lieut. Col. F. under Denzell Hollis Sep 1642, 43
Bingham, Celestine, 13
Bingham, Christopher, 30
Bingham, Robert, 14
Bingley, Richard, Lieut. F. under William Bamfield Sep 1642, 26
Bingley, Richard, Cor. H. under Earl of Stamford Sep 1642, 48
Bird, Jo., Capt. F. under Earl of Stamford Sep 1642, 40
Bird, John, Capt. H. Sep 1642, 49
Birke, Thomas, 21
Biron – *see* Byron
Bishop, Henry, 15
Blackborow, B__, 50
Blackman, John, 53
Blage (usu. Blague), Thomas, Col. F. Dec 1642, list [8] alleges Blage and regiment lost, 58*, 62*
Blake, ___, Ens. F. under Lord Wharton Sep 1642, 40
Blake, John, Capt. of merchant ship *Friendship* Apr 1643, 68
Blake, William, Ens. F. under William Bamfield Sep 1642, 43
Blakistone, William, 16
Bladwell, James, 13
Bland, Francis, Capt. Ens. F. reformado Jun 1642, 30; Lieut. F. under Sir William Fairfax Sep 1642, 45
Bland, Gregory, 31
Bland, Michael, Ens. F. under Sir Nicholas Byron, 1640, 19
Bland, Michael, Capt. F. under Sir William Fairfax Jun 1642, 45
Bland, Michael, Lieut. H. to Robert Baker under William Bamfield Jun 1642, 26

Bland, Richard, Ens. F. under Lord Wharton, Jun 1642, 24; same, Sep 1642, 40
Blanden, Jo., 44
Blankchard, Herbert, 25
Blatchford, Richard, 30
Blewin, Peter, 41
Blith (or Blyth), ___, navy, Capt. of *Vanguard* Dec 1642, 33; Capt. of *Prince Royall* Apr 1643, 67
Blith, Richard jun., navy, Lieut. of *Vanguard* Dec 1642, 33; Capt. of *Mary Rose* Apr 1643, 67
Blodwell, James, 42
Blount, Charles, 25
Blowe, Robert, 40
Bluder, Henry, 19
Blundell, Henry, Ens. F. under Francis Hamond 1640, 21; Capt. Ens. F. reformado 1642, 30; Capt. F. under Thomas Grantham Sep 1642, 44
Blundell, Thomas, 44
Blunt, Charles, 40
Blunt, George, 39
Blunt, John, Ens. F. under Earl of Newport 1640, 10
Blunt, John, Ens. F. under Sir James Hamilton 1640, 20
Blunt, Robert, 30
Bock, James, 40
Bolle, Richard, Lieut. Col. F. under Richard Feilding 1640, 13; Col. F. Dec 1642, list [8] alleges Bolle and regiment lost, 58*, 62*
Bolls, Jo., 29
Bolton, Daniel, 12
Bond, Nicholas, 30
Bond, Richard, 19
Bonner, Jarvis, 52
Bonny, Robert, 10
Bosome (or Bozoone), Thomas, 19
Bossa, Samuell, Lieut. H. reformado Jun 1642, 29; Lieut. H. under Earl of Stamford Sep 1642, 48; Lieut. H. under John Bird, 49. Bossa cannot have been in both Stamford's and Bird's troops, which suggests either another man with his name, or an error in the list.
Boughty, William, 41
Bourcher, William, 26
Bowden, George, Capt. of merchant ship *George of Dover* Apr 1643, 68
Bowdon, ___, Ens. F. under Sir Thomas Culpepper 1640, 16
Bowen, ___, Capt. F. under William Ashburnham Nov 1642, 56*
Bowen, J___, navy, Lieut. of *Entrance* Dec 1642, 33; Capt. of *Entrance* Apr 1643, 67
Bowen, William, Ens. F. under Earl of Essex 1642, 38
Bower (or Bowyler), Francis, Lieut. F. under Thomas Ballard Jun 1642, 25; same, Sep 1642, 45
Bower, Jo., 30

Bower, Robert, 38
Bowermen, Henry, 19
Bowes, ___, Capt. F. under William Vavasour 1640, 17
Bowes, Toby, Capt. F. under Richard Feilding 1640, 21
Bowles, Robert, 13
Boyer, Francis, 14
Boyer, Henry, 15
Boys, John, 12
Brach, Gervase, 25
Bradbury, Francis, 53
Bradford, Barnaby, 9
Bradford, William, 44
Bradley, Walter, 41
Bradshagh, Roger, Lieut. Col. F. under Sir Herbert Price, Dec 1642, 60*
Bradshaw, Richard, 13
Bragge, Thomas, 18
Brakey, Jervis, 50
Bramble, Robert, navy, Commander & Master of *Hinde* Apr 1643, 67
Bramston, Jo., 41
Brand, Jasper, Capt. Ens. F. reformado Jun 1642, 30; Capt. F. under Lord Rochford Sep 1642, 41
Brand, Joseph, 11
Brandling, Ralph, 11
Brandling, Robert, 10
Brandy, Thomas, 45
Brase, ___, 15
Bray, Edward, 21
Braygrave, Thomas, 22
Breckham, James, 44
Bredman, Thomas, 29
Bret, Francis, 21
Brett, Benjamin, 17
Brett (or Britt), Edward, 17
Brett, Jerom, 20
Brewnett, Peter, 16
Bricknell, James, 47
Bridgeman, ___, 16
Bridges, John, Ens. F. under Earl of Peterborough Sep 1642, 39
Bridges, John, Capt. F. under Lord Brook Sep 1642, 42
Bridges, William, Lieut. F. under Lord Wharton Sep 1642, 40
Bridges, William, Lieut. F. under Lord Brooke Sep 1642, 42
Bristol, John Digby 1st Earl of, subscription to levy horse for the King, Jun 1642, 36; horse troops Nov 1642, 57*; Dec 1642, 62*
Briston, Christopher, 51
Brockett, Anthony, 20

Brockett, Edmond, 14
Brockett (or Brockit), William, 13
Broghill, Roger Boyle, Baron Broghill, 23
Brokhaven, John, 34
Brook, William, navy, Capt. of *Providence* Apr 1643, 68
Brookbank, Humphrey, 48
Brooke, Robert Greville 2nd Baron Brooke, Col. F. Sep 1642, 41; Capt. H., 48
Broughton, Daniel, 12
Broughton, John, 41
Broughton, Robert, 15
Brown, John, Col. Dr. Sep 1642, 53
Browne, ___, Capt. F. under Sir Lewis Dyve Nov 1642, 56*
Browne, Edward, Lieut. F. under Lord Wharton Jun 1642, 24; same, Sep 1642, 40
Browne, James, 13
Browne, Jo., Capt. F. reformado 1642, 29
Browne, Jo., Capt. F. under Thomas Ballard Sep 1642, 45
Browne, Sir John, Capt. Dr. under Col. John Brown Sep 1642, 53
Browne, Jo., Ens. F. under William Bamfield 1642, 27; same, Sep 1642, 43
Browne, Jo., Chirurgion to Charles Essex's regiment Sep 1642, 46
Browne, John, Lieut. H. under Arthur Goodwin Sep 1642, 50
Browne, Nicholas, 20
Browne, Thomas, Lieut. F. under Lord Grandison 1640, 12
Browne, Thomas, Lieut. F. to Jeremy Horton under Lord Wharton Jun 1642, 24
Browne, Thomas, Lieut. F. under Thomas Grantham Sep 1642, 44
Browne, William, 40
Browning, Harman, 38
Broxley, Thomas, 11
Brudnell, Thomas, 48
Bruerton, ___, 56*
Brumley, Thomas, 19
Bruse, Robert, 49
Bryan (or O'Brien), Henry, 12
Bucham, William, 53
Bucke, Brutus, 18
Bugslock, William, 51
Bulhead, ___, 56*
Burbeck, Jo., 41
Burges, Dr. ___, 39
Burges, Roger, 21
Burgh, Christopher, Capt. F. under William Bamfield Jun 1642, 26; Capt. F. under Lord Saye, Sep 1642, 40
Burghill, Robert, 20
Burksley, Henry, 43
Burleigh, Jere., 45
Burles, William, 43

Burley, ___, navy, Capt. of *Antelope* Dec 1642, 33
Burley, ___, Capt. F. under Sir Charles Lucas Nov 1642, 56*
Burrell, Bartholomew, 43
Burrell, George, 41
Burrell, James, 46
Burrell, Robert, 48
Burrowes, ___, Capt. F. under Sir John Gooderick Nov 1642, 56*
Burrowes (or Barrowes), Cashea, Capt. F. under Earl of Newport 1640, 10
Burton, Humfrey, Ens. F. under William Bamfield Jun 1642, 26; Lieut. under same Sep 1642, 43
Burwell, George, 20
Burwick, Lodowick, 13
Bury, John, 43
Bury, William, 14
Bushell, Anthony, 16
Bushell, Bridges, 42
Bushell, Thomas, Capt. F. under Sir James Hamilton 1640, 20; Capt. F. reformado 1642, 29
Butcherfield, John, 40
Butler, Francis, 26
Butler, John, Lieut. F. under Sir John Merrick, 15
Butler, John, Capt. F. under Earl of Peterborough Sep 1642, 39
Butler, William, 30
Butrell, Jo., 30
Buttler, ___, 57*
Button, Miles, 15
Button, Thomas, Capt. F. under Sir John Merrick 1640, 15; Capt. Ens. F. reformado 1642, 30
Byron (or Biron), Gilbert, Maj. H. under Sir John Byron Dec 1642, 61*
Byron (or Biron), Sir John, Capt. H. Nov 1642, 57*; horse regiment, Dec 1642, 61*
Byron (or Biron), Sir Nicholas, 19
Byron, Sir Thomas, Maj. H. under Prince of Wales, Capt. of his troop, Nov 1642, 57*; Dec 1642, 60*
Cade, Ambrose, 43
Caldecott, John, 45
Calmady (or Kilmady), Vincent, Capt. under Philip Wharton Jun 1642, 24; Lieut. Col. under Sir John Merrick, Sep 1642, 39
Calton, Duke, 20
Cambridge, 2nd Earl of, *see* James Hamilton
Cannon, Peter, 37
Cantrell, Henry, 40
Capell, Arthur 1st Baron Capel of Hadham, subscription to levy horse for the King, King, Jun 1642, 36; horse troops Nov 1642, 57*; confirmed as having sided with the King Dec 1642, 65
Capell, William, 34

Capper (or Cupper), Thomas, 17
Carde, Thomas, 19
Cardinall, Thomas, 15
Carew – *see also* Carey, Cary
Carew, Edward, 41
Carew, George, 20
Carew, Henry, Capt. F. under Lord Wharton Jun 1642, 24; same, Sep 1642, 40
Carew (or Carry), Sir Mathew, 20
Carey, ___, 56*
Carleton, Thomas, 20
Carlisle, James Hay, 2nd Earl of, confirmed as having sided with the King Dec 1642, 65
Carmichaell, Jo., 51
Carnarvon, Robert Dormer 1st Earl of, subscription to levy horse for the King, Jun 1642, 36; horse regiment mentioned Dec 1642, 61*; confirmed as having sided with the King Dec 1642, 65
Carne, Thomas, 15
Carnock, John, 19
Carre, William, 16
Carrow, Thomas, 17
Carter, Abraham, 39, 49
Carter, John, 12
Carter, Ralph, 41
Carter, Richard, Lieut. F. under Sir Thomas Culpepper 1640, 16; Carter, Richard, Capt. F. reformado 1642, 29
Carwardine, Edward, 40
Carwardine, James, 20
Cary – *see also* Carey, Carew
Cary, ___, Capt. F. under Lord Barrymore 1640, 12
Cary, ___, Capt. F. under Sir William Ogle 1640, 18
Cary, Greevile, Ens. F. under Thomas Lunsford 1640, 17
Cary (or Carew), Horatio, Capt. F. under Sir James Hamilton 1640, 19; Capt. F. under William Bamfield Jun 1642, 26; Maj. H. under Sir William Waller Sep 1642, 47, 49
Case, Henry, 39
Casie, William, 41
Castillion, Poynton, 17
Cattorill, Thomas, 43
Cavaler, Isack, 49
Cavendish, Charles, Col. H., commanded Duke of York's regiment; Dec 1642, 60*
Caworth, ___, 26
Chadwick, Lewis, 53
Chalise (or Challice, Challys), Isaac, Provost Marshall to Sir John Merrick's regiment 1640, 15; Lieut. F. reformado Jun 1642, 30; Lieut. F. under Thomas Grantham Sep 1642, 44
Chalwell, Phillip, 17

Chambers, John, 40
Chambers, Robert, 37
Chapline, Thomas, 16
Chaune, Arthur, 11
Chayton, Henry, 9
Cheney, William, Lieut. F. under Henry Lunsford 1640, 17; Lieut. F. reformado 1642, 30
Cheney, William, Cor. H. under Earl of Peterborough Sep 1642, 47
Chester, Edward, 17
Cheviers, Jeremy, 16
Chichester, Ch__, 51
Chidley, Christopher, 45
Cholmley (or Cholmlie), Sir Henry, 43
Chonnocke, John, 19
Chriswell, Henry, 16
Chudleigh, Christopher, 25
Chudleigh, James, 9
Churchman, Thomas, 43
Chyne, John, 16
Cicill, Benjamin, 44
Clare, John Holles 2nd Earl of, confirmed as having sided with the King Dec 1642, 65
Clarke, Thomas, Capt. of merchant ship *Leopard* Apr 1643, 68
Clarke, ___, Quart. H. under Ed. Ayscough Sep 1642, 49
Clarke, Francis, Lieut. Col. F. reformado Jun 1642, 29; Lieut. Col. F. under Thomas Grantham Sep 1642, 44
Clarke, George, Lieut. F. under Earl of Essex Sep 1642, 38
Clarke, Samuel, Cor. H. under Henry Ireton Sep 1642, 51
Cleare, John, 42
Clement, Thomas, 43
Cleyton, Randoll, 29
Clifton, John, Lieut. F. under Jerom Brett 1640, 20; Capt. Ens. F. reformado Jun 1642, 30; Lieut. F. under Earl of Stamford Sep 1642, 40
Clifton, Laurence, 40
Cobb, Francis, 21
Cobb, Isaac, 11
Cockain, Joseph, 29
Cockaine, John, 50
Cockram, Edward, 38
Codrington, Nicholas, 14
Codrington, William, 20
Colbie, Thomas, 11
Cole, John, 17
Coleby, Thomas, 26
Coleman, William, 42

Index 87

Colesfoote, ___, 56*
Colield, Lambert, 19
Colle, Thomas, 34
Collingwood, Henry, Ens. F. under Earl of Stamford, Sep 1642, 40
Collingwood, Henry, Ens. F. under Thomas Ballard, Sep 1642, 45
Collins, Digory, Capt. F. under Jerom Brett 1640, 20; Maj. under Sir Ralph Dutton, list [8] reports as dead, hurt or captured Dec 1642, 62*
Collins, Marmaduke, 12
Collins, Thomas, 21
Collugno, Owen, 17
Compton, Richard, 49
Compton, Thomas, 44
Coney, ___, 55*
Coningsby (or Conisby), Robert, 13
Consiby, Thomas, 21
Constable, Robert, Capt. of merchant ship *Ruth* Dec 1642, 34; same, Apr 1643, 69
Constable, Sir William, Col. F. Sep 1642, 44; 46
Coo, Thomas, 44
Cook, Thomas, navy, Commander & Master of *Starre* Apr 1643, 69
Cooke, Edward, 43
Cooke, Francis, 15
Cooke, George, 10
Cooke, Henry, 11
Cooke, Michael, 30
Cooke, Nicholas, 37
Cooke, Phillip, 12
Cooke, Richard, 19
Cooker, William, 50
Cooney, John, 12
Cooper, Conyers, Corp. H. under Lord Wharton Jun 1642, 23; Cor. H. under Walter Long Sep 1642, 51
Cooper (or Couper), Marmaduke, Cor. H. under Alexander Nayrne Jun 1642, 23; Lieut. H. under Lord St. John Sep 1642, 48
Coote, Thomas, 20
Cope, Henry, 25
Cope (or Coape), William, 10
Copley, Lionell, 37
Coppin, William, Capt. of merchant ship *Elizabeth and Anne* Apr 1643, 68
Coquinx, Anthony, 10
Corbet, Vincent, 52
Corby, ___, 40
Corey (or Cory), Humfrey, Lieut. F. under Sir James Hamilton 1640, 20; Colonel's Capt. F. reformado, 1642, 30
Cornewallis, Thomas, 20
Corney (or Cornay), William, Lieut. F. under Sir James Hamilton 1640, 20; Lieut.

F. reformado 1642, 30
Cornwall, Humfrey, 20
Cosbie, Arnold, 40
Cosworth, ___, Ens. F. under Richard Feilding 1640, 21
Cosworth, Samuel, Cor. H. under Anthony Mildmay Sep 1642, 50
Cotsforth, Ralph, 42
Cotterell, Roger, 42
Cotton, ___, 42
Court, Jo. 43
Courtney, Edward, 11
Courtney, William 13
Couse, William, 49
Coutop, ___, 44
Coventry, Thomas 2nd Baron Coventry, subscription to levy horse for the King, Jun 1642, 36; confirmed as having sided with the King Dec 1642, 65
Cowgrave, Francis, 17
Cowse, William, 30
Cox, William, 10
Coyshe (or Coshe), Jo., Quart. H. under Sir Faithful Fortescue Jun 1642, 23; Lieut. H. under George Thompson Sep 1642, 49
Cracroft (or Cratroft), John, Lieut. F. under Richard Feilding 1640, 21; Lieut. F. under Earl of Essex 1642, 38
Craft, Thomas, Commander of fire ship *Andrew and John* Apr 1643, 68
Crane, ___, Capt. F. under Lord Grandison Nov 1642, 56*
Crane, William, Corp. H. under John Hurry Jun 1642, 23
Cranley, Benjamin, navy, Capt. of *Leopard* Apr 1643, 67
Crant, Thomas, 31
Crawford, Ludovic Lindsay 16th Earl of, horse troops Nov 1642, 57*; horse troop under Duke of York, 61*
Crawley, William, a 'chiefe' (Jun, reformado); then 'principall' (Sep), 'conductor of the amunition, draught horses and traine of Artillery'; 31, 38
Crish, Obadiah, 52
Crispe, Peter, Lieut. F. to Adam Cunningham under Charles Essex, Jun 1642, 26; Capt. F. under Earl of Stamford Sep 1642, 40
Croft (or Crofts), Robert, 10
Croker, John, 48
Crompton, Henry, 11
Cromwell, Oliver, Capt. H. Sep 1642, 52
Cromwell, Oliver, Ens. F. under Philip Wharton Jun 1642, 24; Cor. H. under Lord St. John Sep 1642, 48. Son of Oliver Cromwell.
Cromwell, Thomas, 1st Viscount Lecale, 'Lord Viscount Cromwell', Dec 1642, 60*
Crooker, Henry, 12
Cropley, Edward, 16
Crosse, Richard, 48
Crosse, Thomas, 38

Crow, Christopher, Quart. F. under Charles Essex Jun 1642, 32; Lieut. F. under, same, Sep 1642, 45
Crow, Henry, 29
Crow, Stephen, 29
Crowe, Christopher, 21
Cruttenden, Bevill, 39
Culpepper, Sir Thomas, 15
Cumberland, Henry Clifford 5th Earl of, subscription to levy horse for the King, Jun 1642, 35; has raised horse and foot Nov 1642, 57*; confirmed as being with the King Dec 1642, 65
Cunningham (or Coningham), Adam, Lieut. Col. F. under Charles Essex Jun 1642, 26; same, Sep 1642, 45
Dabscoate, Thomas, 19
Daily, John, 42
Daldorne, Henry, 51
Dallison, Sir Thomas, horse troop under Duke of York mentioned Dec 1642, 61*
Dallochin, James, 13
Danby, Sir Thomas, Lieut. Col. F. under Sir John Belasyse, list [8] reports as dead, hurt or captured Dec 1642, 62*
Dane, Michael, 43
Daniell, John, 19
Dansk, Ralph, Capt. of merchant ship *Charity* Apr 1643, 68
Danyell (or Danil), Thomas, 11
Darcey (or Darey), John, navy, Lieut. of *Antelope* 1640, 22; Lieut. of *Charles* 1642, 33
Davies, Charles, 42
Davies, Thomas, 42
Davies, W__, Lieut. Col. to Earl of Essex 1642, 38.
Davis, John, 41
Davis, Robert, Lieut. F. under Sir John Dougless 1640, 20
Davis (or Davies), Robert, Ens. F. under Thomas Ballard 1642, 25; Lieut. F. under same, Sep 1642, 45
Davis, Rolland, 16
Davis, William, Maj. to Sir John Merricke 1640, 15
Davison, Alexander, 51
Davyes, Robert, 20
Dawson, Charles, Capt. to Marquess of Hamilton 1640, 18
Dawson, Charles, Capt. to Lord Kerry 1642, 25
Dawson, Stephen, 10
Day, William, 51
Deane, Nicholas, 21
Deane, Stephen, 44
De Boyes, ___, Lieutenant General, Capt. firelocks 1642, 38
De Boyes (or Duboyce), Philibert Emanuel, Controler of the Ordinance and chiefe Engineer, reformado, Jun 1642, 31; Lieut. Gen. of the Ordnance, Sep 1642, 37; 46

De Gennis (or Degennes), John, Cor. H. reformado Jun 1642, 29; Lieut. H. under Henry Ireton Sep 1642, 51
De La Blancheur, J__, 51
De La Hay, Joh., Lieut. Capt. H. under Arthur Evelin Sep 1642, 49
Deering, Edward, Lieut. F. under Lord Rochford Sep 1642, 41
Deight, ___, 19
Delamyne, Henry, 31
Delasley, Theodore, 14
Denby, ___, 56*
Denn, William, 19
Denny, Sir Ed., 25
Derby, James Stanley 7th Earl of, 57*
Derickbore, Albion, 43
Dethick, William, 20
Devereux, Nicholas, 39
Devonshire, William Cavendish 3rd Earl of, subscription to levy horse for the King, Jun 1642, 35; confirmed as having sided with the King Dec 1642, 65
Dewz (properly D'Ewes), Richard, Lieut. Col. under Richard Bolle, list [8] reports as dead, hurt or captured Dec 1642, 62*
Dibdale, Nicholas, 42
Dick, Lodwick, Capt. of merchant ship *Golden Lion of Leech* Apr 1643, 68
Digby, George, Baron Digby, horse troops Nov 1642, 57*; Dec 1642, 62*
Digby, Sir John (of Gayhurst), Lieut. Col. H. under Lord Grandison Nov 1642, 55*; Dec 1642, 60*
Dillon, ___, Capt. F. under Thomas Lunsford 1640, 17
Dillion, Jo., Capt. F. reformado 1642, 29
Dillon, Nathanael, Lieut. F. under Earl of Northumberland 1640, 9
Dillon, Thomas, 4th Viscount, Maj. F. under Lord Taaffe, Dec 1642, 58*
Dimock – *see also* Dymock
Dimock, ___, Capt. H. Sep 1642, 49
Dingley, Francis, 30
Dingley, John, 51
Disbrow, John, 52
Disney, Edward, 21
Dives (usu. Dyve), Sir Lewis, Col. F. Nov 1642, 56*; Dec 1642, list [8] alleges regiment lost, 58*
Dix, Humfrey, 40
Dlausherd [*sic*], Herbert, 47
Dobson, Isaac, 40
Dobson, Miles, 41
Dodsworth, Sir Edward, Commissary of the Muster, reformado, Jun 1642, 30; Commissary of the Horse, Sep 1642, 37
Don, Daniel, 10
Donnell (or Doneill), ___, 16
Dorisla, Dr. Isaack, Advocate of the Army Sep 1642, 37; 46

Dormer, ___, Capt. F. under Sir John Beaumont, Dec 1642, 60*

Dorset, Edward Sackville 4th Earl of, subscription to levy horse for the King, Jun 1642, 35; confirmed as having sided with the King Dec 1642, 65

Dothwait, William, Lieut. F. to Agmondisham Muschamp under Lord Kerry 1642, 25

Doughty, Michael, 20

Douglas, ___, Capt. F. under Lord Taaffe Nov 1642, 55*

Douglas, Alexander, Maj. H. under Edwin Sands Sep 1642, 47; 50

Dougless, Sir John, Col. F. 1640, 20

Dover, Henry Carey 1st Earl of, subscription to levy horse for the King, Jun 1642, 35; confirmed as having sided with the King Dec 1642, 65

Dover, Thomas, 30

Dowes, Richard, Lieut. F. under George Goring 1640, 11

Dowet (or Doyet), Francis, Lieut. H. under Sir Faithful Fortescue Jun 1642, 23; Capt. H. Sep 1642, 49

Downcham, Jo., 50

Downing, Calibut, 43

Downing, George, 'Comisary of the victuals in the army' 1642, 30

Dowse, Richard, Capt. F. under Earl of Northumberland 1640, 9

Dowthwayte, William, Cor. H. reformado 1642, 29

Drake, Jo., Capt. F. reformado Jun 1642, 29; Maj. F. under Lord Mandeville Sep 1642, 42

Drake, Thomas, 41

Draper, Mathew or Nathaniel, Capt. H., 'Captain to the Generals Troop of 50. Carbines', Sep 1642, 39, 49. The list gives Draper alternative first names; it is not known which is correct.

Draper, Thomas, 20

Draper, William 21

Drewell, George, 17

Driver, William, Capt. of merchant ship *Prosperous* Dec 1642, 34; same, Apr 1643, 68

Drury, Edward, 18

Dugdaile, Jo., 44

Dulbeir (usu. Dalbier), John, Quart. Gen. H., 37; Capt. H. Sep 1642, 50

Duncombe, Sir Edward, Col. Dr., Dec 1642, 61*

Dungan, John, 38

Dunlas, George, 53

Dunsmore, Francis Leigh 1st Baron Dunsmore, subscription to levy horse for the King, Jun 1642, 36; Dec 1642, 62*; confirmed as having sided with the King Dec 1642, 65

Durdo, Thomas, 43

Dutton, Phillip, 30

Dutton, Sir Ralph, Col. F. Dec 1642, list [8] alleges Dutton and regiment lost, 58*; 62*

Dymock – *see also* Dimock

Dymmocke, Edward, 16

Dymocke (or Dimock), Humphrey, Capt. Ens. F. reformado Jun 1642, 30; Lieut. F. under Lord Rochford Sep 1642, 41

Dymocke (or Dymock, Dymmocke), Thomas, Capt. F. under Sir Thomas Glemham, 1640, 14; Maj. F. reformado 1642, 29

Ealsinan, John, 51

Earle, Sir Walter, 50

Earnlesse, John, 12

Eaton, John, 12

Echlyn, Henry, 21

Edson, Henry, 38

Edwards, Alexander, 38

Edwards, John, Capt. F. under Earl of Northumberland 1640, 9

Edwards, John, Lieut. F. under Sir John Merrick 1640, 15; Capt. F. under same, 1642, 39

Eggleston, ___, 42

Eldred, Benjamin, 21

Eliot, Thomas, Quart. H. under Robert Burrell Sep 1642, 48

Elliot (or Elecot), Bartholomew, Lieut. F. under Charles Essex Jun 1642, 26; same, Sep 1642, 45

Elliot, George, 41

Elliot, Jonathan, 42

Elliot, Richard, 11

Elliot, Thomas, Lieut. H. under Francis Thompson Sep 1642, 52

Ellis, Thomas, 12

Elrington, John, 19

Elsing (or Elsinge), Christopher, Ens. F. under Sir Nicholas Byron 1640, 19; Capt. Ens. F. reformado 1642, 30

Emerson, William, 40

Erreny, Bullen, 20

Errington, John, Lieut. F. under Richard Feilding, 1640, 21

Errington, Jo., Capt. F. reformado 1642, 29. May be the man above, but a great many of the Errington family participated in the conflicts of the 1640s, so identification of this officer is not certain.

Esline, James, 14

Essex, Charles, Col. F. Jun 1642, 26; Sep 1642, 45

Essex, Robert Devereux 3rd Earl of, 'Captain General', 'His Excellency' 1642, 37, 38

Essex, Thomas, 41

Essex, Sir William, 46

Eure, Thomas, 44

Evane, Thomas, Capt. of merchant ship *Scipio* Apr 1643, 68

Evans, Thomas, 51

Evelin, Arthur, 49

Evers, Compton, 16

Evert, William, 16

Exton, John, Ens. F. under Sir Nicholas Byron 1640, 19; Lieut. F. reformado

1642, 30
Fairfax, Francis, Capt. F. reformado Jun 1642, 29; Maj. F. under Earl of Peterborough, Sep 1642, 39
Fairfax, Sir William, 45
Falkland, Lucius Carey 2nd Viscount, subscription to levy horse for the King, Jun 1642, 36; Dec 1642, 62*
Farley, Cuthbert, 42
Farnes, Joseph, 40
Farr, Hugh, 23
Farrew, Humfrey, 17
Farrier, ___, 55*
Farrington, David, 10
Farrington, Robert, 46
Fauckner, John, 22
Faulconbridge (or Fauconberg), Thomas Belasyse 1st Baron, subscription to levy horse for the King, Jun 1642, 36; confirmed as having sided with the King Dec 1642, 65
Feilding, Edward, Lieut. Col. F. under Marquess of Hamilton 1640, 18; Maj. H. under Henry Wilmot Dec 1642, 61*
Feilding, Basil, Viscount Feilding, 'Lord Feilding', Col. H. Sep 1642, 47, 48
Feilding, Richard, 13, 21
Fennour, Robert, 30
Fenton, Sir William, 30
Fenwick, John, 44
Fenwicke, Tristram, 9
Ferrer, Constance, Capt. F. under Sir William Ogle 1640, 18; Capt. F. under Charles Essex Jun 1642, 26; Maj. F. under Earl of Stamford Sep 1642, 40
Ferrer (Ferries), Henry, 17
Ferrors, Thomas, 20
Fidler, ___, 57*
Finch, ___, Ens. F. under William Vavasour 1640, 17
Finch, Jonathan, Quart. H. under John Bird Sep 1642, 49
Fines, Edward, 53
Fines, Francis, 50
Fines, Henry, 50
Fines, John, 51
Fines, Nathaniel, 50
Fisher, ___, Capt. F. under Earl of Newcastle Nov 1642, 55*
Fisher, ___, Capt. F. under Henry Hastings Nov 1642, 55*
Fisher, Henry, Provost Marshall under Marquess of Hamilton 1640, 19; same under Sir William Fairfax, Sep 1642, 45
Fisher, John, Lieut. F. under Jerom Brett 1640, 20
Fisher, John, Lieut. F. under Sir Henry Cholmley Sep 1642, 43
Fisher, William, 20
Fitch, Thomas, 42

Fitz, Thomas, 45
Fitzgerald, John, 12
Fitzhughes (or Fitshues), Francis, Capt. Ens. F. reformado Jun 1642, 30; Lieut. F. under Lord Wharton Sep 1642, 40
Fitzjames, John, 21
Flawes, James, Commander of fire ship *Lyon of London* Apr 1643, 68
Fleetwood, ___, Capt. F. under Sir William Ogle 1640, 18
Fleetwood, ___, Lieut. F. under Sir William Ogle 1640, 18
Fleetwood, ___, Capt. F. under Earl of Newcastle Nov 1642, 55*
Fleming, ___, Ens. F. under Lord Mandeville Sep 1642, 42
Fleming, Ch., Lieut. H. under Robert Kirle Sep 1642, 52
Fleming, Ed., Cor. H. under John Fleming Sep 1642, 50
Fleming, John, Capt. H. Sep 1642, 50
Fletcher, John, 19
Flood, John, 30
Floyd – *see also* Lloyd
Floyd, ___, Capt. F. under Lord Taaffe Nov 1642, 55*
Fludd (or Lloyd), Charles, 9
Fog, John, navy, Capt. of *Garland* 1640, 22; Dec 1642, 33
Fog, Robert, navy, Lieut. of *Garland* 1640, 22; Dec 1642, 33
Food, John, 20
Fook – *see also* Fowke
Fook (or Fowke), Francis jun., Quart. H. under John Trenchard Jun 1642, 24; Lieut. F. under Thomas Ballard Sep 1642, 45
Fook (or Foukes), Francis sen., Capt. F. under Thomas Ballard Jun 1642, 25; same, Sep 1642, 45
Fooks, James, 42
Foord, George, Lieut. F. under Richard Feilding 1640, 21
Forboys, Alexander, 37
Ford, ___, Capt. F. under Sir Charles Lucas Nov 1642, 56*
Forster, ___, 57*
Fortescue, Sir Faithfull, Capt. of H. Jun 1642, 23; Lieut. Col. F. under Earl of Peterborough, Sep 1642, 39; Capt. H. Sep 1642, 52; Lieut. Col. under Viscount Kilmurrey Nov 1642, 56*; Dec 1642, 60*. His horse troop famously defected to the King during the battle of Edgehill.
Fortescue, Thomas, 23
Foster, Charles, 10
Foster, John, 45
Fotherby (or Fothersby), Henry, Capt. F. under Henry Wentworth 1640, 14; Capt. F. reformado 1642, 30
Fountain, Charles, 51
Fountaine, Ornall, 39
Fowke – *see also* Fook
Fowke, John, 38
Fowler, ___, 56*

Fowles, Edward, Lieut. F. under Sir Jacob Astley 1640, 11
Fowles, Edward, Ens. F. under Thomas Lunsford 1640, 17
Fowles (or Fowlis), William, Ens. F. under Thomas Ballard Jun 1642, 25; same, Sep 1642, 45
Fox, ___, 33
Fox, Charles, 17
Fox, John, Ens. F. under Earl of Newport 1640, 10
Fox, John, Capt. F. under Richard Feilding 1640, 21
Fox, Robert, 22
Framton, William, 50
France, William, 45
Francis, John, 43
Francis, Richard, 21
Francklin, James, 38
Franouth, Humphrey, 43
Freake, Jo., 24
Frederick, William, 45
Freeman, ___, Chaplain to William Bamfield's regiment Sep 1642, 44
Freeman, Ralph, Lieut. F. under Sir Nicholas Byron 1640, 19
Frenchfield, ___, 33
Frodsham Edward, 38
Frodsham, Henry, 44
Frost, ___, Capt. F. under Earl of Newcastle Nov 1642, 55*
Frost, Walter, 'Commissary of the Victuals of England' reformado Jun 1642, 30
Fryer, ___, 55*
Fuller, Chenie, 51
Fuller, George, 11
Fulwood, George, Capt. Ens. F. reformado Jun 1642, 30; Lieut. F. under Sir Henry Cholmley Sep 1642, 43
Furbush, Thomas, 56*
Gamble, Herald, 30
Gamblin, William, 20
Gandey, Robert, 20
Gardiner, James, 10
Gardiner, Jer., 40
Gardiner, Nicholas, 31
Gardiner, Thomas, 19
Garfeild, Henry, 21
Garfoot, William, Ens. F. under Thomas Ballard Jun 1642, 25; same Sep 1642, 45
Garrard, Nethermill, 44
Garret, John, 40
Garrett (or Garret), Thomas, Lieut. F. under Sir Nicholas Byron 1640, 19; Capt. Ens. F. reformado 1642, 30
Garth, Nicholas, 43
Garth (or Garts), Ralph, Ens. F. under William Bamfield Jun 1642, 26; Lieut. under

same Sep 1642, 43
Gates, John, 42
Gaudy, Francis, 12
Gaudy, Thomas, 29
Gaulter, William 19
Gay, Francis, Ens. F. under Sir Jacob Astley 1640, 11; Waggon Master to Thomas Ballard's regiment Jun 1642, 31; Lieut. F. under Thomas Grantham Sep 1642, 44
Gay, Richard, 44
Gerard, Sir Gilbert of Halsall, younger brother of Col. Charles Gerard. Lieut. Col. F. to Lord Molyneux, reported dead after Edgehill, 63*
Gerrard (or Garrat), Charles, 11
Gerrard, Sir Gilbert, 1st Baronet, Treasurer at War Sep 1642, 37
Gerrard, Hugh, 14
Gibb, Henry, 51
Gibbons, ___, Capt. F. under Lord Wharton Sep 1642, 40
Gibbons (or Guibon), Deverex, Lieut. F. under Sir Jacob Astley, 11; Waggon Master General to Lord Wharton's regiment Jun 1642, 31
Gibbons, Robert, Provost Marshall to Thomas Grantham's regiment Sep 1642, 44
Gibbs, ___, Maj. F. under Thomas Lunsford 1640, 17
Gibbs, Higham, Preacher to Earl of Newport's regiment, 10
Gibbs, Richard, Capt. F. under Thomas Grantham Sep 1642, 44
Gibbs, Thomas, Capt. F. under Jerom Brett 1640, 20
Gibbs, William, Maj. F. under Jerom Brett 1640, 20
Gibson, Richard, 15
Gifford, ___, Capt. F. under Lord Barrymore 1640, 12
Gifford, George, Lieut. F. under Sir William Fairfax Sep 1642, 45
Gifford, John, Maj. F. under Francis Hamond 1640, 21
Gifford, Lewis, Lieut. F. under Earl of Northumberland 1640, 9
Gifford, Thomas, 20
Giggins, Symon, 43
Gilborne, Thomas, 30
Gilby, Immanuel, Maj. F., list [8] reports as dead, hurt or captured Dec 1642, 62*. The pamphlet incorrectly states that Gilby was Maj. to John Belasyse; in fact, it was to William Eure.
Gill, William, 49
Gillmore, Charles, 17
Ginnings, Thomas, 42
Gittings, ___, 40
Glassington, John, 20
Gleane, Peter, 18
Glemham (or Glenham, Glentham), Sir Thomas, Col. F. 1640, 14; Nov 1642, 55*; Dec 1642, 60*
Godderd, James, 48
Godfery, Francis, 14
Godfrey, John, 20

Index 97

Goffe, Edmund, 10
Goldsborow, ___, 39
Goldsmith, Daniel, 21
Goldsmith, David, 45
Golledge, Thomas, 40
Goodrich, John, 20
Gooderick (or Gotherick), Sir John, Col. F. Nov 1642, 56*; horse troop, Nov 1642, 57*; Dec 1642, 60*. List [7] incorrectly names him as 'George'.
Goodlad, Nathanel, navy, Capt. of *Victory* Apr 1643, 67
Goodrick, Daniel, 25
Goodwin, ___, Lieut. under Sir Henry Cholmley Sep 1642, 43
Goodwin, Arthur, Capt. H. Sep 1642, 50
Goodwin, Edward, Capt. Ens. reformado Jun 1642, 30
Goodwin, Jasper, Ens. F. under Lord Mandeville Sep 1642, 42
Goodwin, Robert, 'Commissary of the fixed Magazine' reformado, Jun 1642, 30
Goodwin (or Goodwine), Robert, Ens. F. under Sir Thomas Culpepper 1640, 16; Ens. F. under Thomas Ballard Jun 1642, 25
Goodwin, Robert, Capt. F. under Lord Mandeville Sep 1642, 42
Goodwin, Thomas, Ens. F. under Lord Mandeville, Sep 1642, 42
Gordon, Nathaniel, 53
Gore, [Doyley], Col. Dr., Dec 1642, 61*. In fact the name should be 'Gower': the list states that the officer's brother was High Sheriff of Yorkshire, e.g. Sir Thomas Gower 2nd Baronet, who served 1641-42. Gower's first name is provided by the Collins Peerage of 1812, vol. II p.445.
Gore, Thomas, Corp. H. under Francis Dowett Sep 1642, 49
Gorge, John, 44
Goring, George, 11
Goubourne, Thomas, 13
Gourd, Richard, 51
Graden, James, 42
Grain, Robert, 44
Grandison, William Villiers 2nd Viscount, Col. H. & F. 1640, 11; Lieut. Gen. F. Nov 1642, 55*; horse troop Nov 1642, 57*; Dec 1642, 60*; horse regiment mentioned Dec 1642, 61*
Grant, Arthur, 17
Grantham, Francis, 44
Grantham, Thomas, Col. F. Sep 1642, 44; 46
Gratwick, Thomas, 48
Gratwicke, Jo., 30
Gravenor, Edward, 41
Gray – *see also* Grey
Gray, ___, Capt. F. under Lord Barrymore, 1640, 12
Gray of Ruthyn, Charles Longueville 12th Baron Gray, subscription to levy horse for the King, Jun 1642, 36
Gray, Edward, Capt. F. under George Goring 1640, 11

Gray, Edward, Ens. F. under Francis Hamond 1640, 21
Gray, Ed., Lieut. F. to Elias Struice under Lord Wharton, Jun 1642, 24
Gray, Ed., Corp. H. under William St. Leger, Jun 1642, 24
Gray, Edw., Capt. H. under Earl of Stamford, Sep 1642, 40
Gray, Ferdinando, Quart. F. to Francis Hamond's regiment 1640, 21; Quart. F. to Earl of Stamford's regiment, Sep 1642, 40
Gray, James, Ens. F. under Earl of Stamford Sep 1642, 40
Gray, James, Capt. F. under Sir William Constable Sep 1642, 44
Gray, Mathew, Capt. F. under Francis Hamond 1640, 21
Greatrix, Richard, 12
Green (or Greve), Anthony, Capt. F. under Marquess of Hamilton 1640, 19; Maj. F. under earl of Northampton, mentioned by list [8] Dec 1642, 60*. That list does not supply the Major's first name, but it is known from other sources as Anthony, which matches him to the 1640 captain.
Green, Ed., Ens. H. to Jeremy Horton under Lord Wharton Jun 1642, 24
Greene, John, Lieut. H. under Robert Burrell Sep 1642, 48
Greene, Thomas, Carriage Master to Lord St. John's regiment Sep 1642, 41
Greene, William, Lieut. F. under Sir Thomas Glemham 1640, 14
Grenvile, Richard, 51
Gresham, Paul, Quart. H. reformado Jun 1642, 29; Quart. carbines to Sir Philip Stapleton under Earl of Essex, Sep 1642, 39
Grevill, Foulk, 48
Grey – *see also* Gray
Grey, Edward, Col. Dr., younger brother of Parliamentarian William, Lord Grey of Werke, regiment mentioned Dec 1642, 61*
Grey, Francis, 48
Grey, Thomas, Lord Grey of Groby, 47, 48
Griffen (or Griffith), Conyers, 18
Griffin, Thomas, 40
Griffith, Henry, 30
Griffith, John, 16
Griffith, Robert, 17
Grimes, James, 39
Grimes, Mark, Capt. F. under Lord Robartes Sep 1642, 42
Grimes, Mark, Ens. F. under Lord Robartes Sep 1642, 42. It is not clear if there were two identically-named men in the regiment, or if this was a list or printing error.
Groome, Benjamin, 42
Grove, John, 20
Grover, Francis, 11
Grover, Thomas, 25
Gue, Hugh, 18
Gunter, John, 48
Gurney, Henry, 44
Gwalter, Thomas, Corp. H. under John Trenchard 1642, 24
Gwalter, Thomas, Capt. Ens. F. reformado 1642, 30

Gwyn, ___, 12
Gyles, ___, 55*
Hackluyt (Hakluit), Edward, Lieut. F. under Sir William Ogle 1640, 18; Lieut. F. under Sir William Constable Sep 1642, 44
Haddock, ___, navy, Capt. of *Anthelop* Apr 1643, 67
Hadon, Edmund, 51
Hakriger, ___, 33
Hale, John, 51
Hale, Michael, 51
Hales, Charles, 13
Hales, Edward, 14
Halford, Nicholas, 39
Hall, Francis, Lieut. F. under Charles Essex Jun 1642, 26
Hall, Francis, Lieut. F. under Charles Essex Sep 1642, 45
Hall, Francis, Capt. F. under Charles Essex Sep 1642, 45. It is not clear if there were two identically-named men in the regiment, or if this was a list or printing error. Either way, one of these individuals must be the lieutenant listed in June.
Hambden (usu. Hampden), John, 46
Hambleton, Archibald, 53
Hamilton, James 3rd Marquess of Hamilton and 2nd Earl of Cambridge, 1640, 18; subscription to levy horse for the King, Jun 1642, 35; confirmed as being with the King Dec 1642, 65
Hamilton, Sir James, 19
Hamlon, Robert, 20
Hamond, Edward, 21
Hamond, Francis, 21
Hamond, John, Ens. F. under Earl of Newport 1640, 10
Hamond, John, Capt. H. Sep 1642, 49
Hamond, Robert, Lieut. Col. F. under Francis Hamond 1640, 21; Capt. F. under Lord Kerry 1642, 24
Hamond, Thomas, 50
Hampson, George, 43
Hampson, Robert, 40
Hane, Joakin, 38
Hannam, James, 40
Hanson, Robert, 30
Harcourt, Walter, Quart. F. under Richard Feilding 1640, 21; Quart. H. under Walter Long Sep 1642, 51
Harcus, James, 40
Harding, Hugh, 38
Harding, John, 52
Harecourt, ___, 44
Hardy, Jo., Ens. F. under Thomas Ballard Jun 1642, 25; same, Sep 1642, 45
Harlocke, George, 43

Harris, Leonard, 34
Harris, Nathaniel, 44
Harrison, James, 39
Harrow, Charles, 39
Hart, Jo., 43
Hartridge (or Hartrigg), George, Ens. F. under Sir Nicholas Byron 1640, 19; Lieut. F. under Earl of Peterborough Sep 1642, 39
Harvie, John, 41
Harvie, Robert, 44
Haselwood, John, Capt. F. under Charles Essex Sep 1642, 45
Haslewood, John, Lieut. F. under Sir Jacob Astley 1640, 11
Haselwrick (usu. Haselrig), Sir Arthur, 50
Hastings, Henry, Col. F. Nov 1642, 55*; Dec 1642, 60*; regiment mentioned, 61*
Hastings, Ferdinando, Viscount Hastings, 'Lord Hastings' (son of Henry 5th Earl of Huntingdon)? Identification uncertain, 48
Hastings, Thomas, 38
Hatch, ___, navy, Capt. of *Henrietta Maria* Dec 1642, 33
Hatcher, Henry, Ens. F. under Richard Feilding 1640, 21
Hatcher, Henry Lieut. H. under Anthony Mildmay Sep 1642, 50
Hatcher, Thomas, Capt. H. Sep 1642, 52
Haward, Arnold, 49
Hawkins, Leonard, Ens. F. under Charles Essex Jun 1642, 26; same, Sep 1642, 45
Hawkins, Stephen, Capt. F. under Jerom Brett 1640, 20; Lieut. Col. under Sir Ralph Dutton, list [8] reports as dead, hurt or captured Dec 1642, 62*
Haynes, Hopton, 31
Haynes, Thomas, 40
Haywood, Arnold, 29
Hearne, George, 9
Heaslewood, John, 20
Heithley, James, 53
Hemert, Walraven, 45
Hemings, ___, Capt. F. under Earl of Newcastle Nov 1642, 55*
Hemings (or Hemens) Jo., Ens. F. to Constance Ferrer under Charles Essex, Jun 1642, 26; Lieut. F. under Earl of Stamford Sep 1642, 40
Hemsley, ___, 12
Hender, William, 42
Henery, Ralph, 23
Henise, Charles, 12
Herbert, William, Capt. F. under Sir John Merrick 1640, 15; Maj. F. under same, 1642, 39
Herdine, John, 38
Herne, Robert, 14
Hertford, William Seymour 1st Marquess of, subscription to levy horse for the King Jun 1642, 35; has raised horse and foot Nov 1642, 57*; confirmed as having sided with the King Dec 1642, 65

Hewet – *see also* Huet
Hewet, William, Lieut. F. to Constance Ferrer under Charles Essex, Jun 1642, 26; Lieut. F. under Earl of Stamford Sep 1642, 40
Heyden, William, Ens. F. under Lord Wharton Jun 1642, 24; same, Sep 1642, 40
Heyford, Anthony, 38
Heys, Walter, 42
Hickman, Thomas, Capt. F. under Lord Brooke Sep 1642, 42
Hickman, Thomas, Cor. H. under Lord Willoughby Sep 1642, 48
Hickmar, Elias, 18
Hickson, William, 38
Hidden (or Hiddon), Roger, Lieut. F. under Sir John Dougless 1640, 20, Lieut. F. reformado 1642, 30
Hide, David, 15
Higgins, Henry, Ens. F. under Thomas Ballard Jun 1642, 25; same, Sep 1642, 45
Higgins, Thomas, 43
Higham, George, Provost Master General to Lord Wharton's regiment, Jun 1642, 31; Provost Marshall to same, Sep 1642, 41
Higham (or Heigham), John, Lieut. F. under Henry Wentworth 1640, 14; Capt. F. reformado 1642, 30
Hilderson (or Hillersden), John, Ens. F. under Earl of Northumberland 1640, 10; Capt. Ens. F. reformado Jun 1642, 30; Capt. F. under Lord St. John Sep 1642, 41
Hill, ___, navy, Lieut. of *Lyon* Dec 1642, 33
Hill, ___, Capt. F. under Lord Taaffe Nov 1642, 55*
Hill, Philip, navy, Capt. of *Providence* 1640, 22.
Hill, R__, navy, Capt. *Tenth Whelp* Apr 1643, 67
Hill, Thomas, 21
Hillyard, ___, 56*
Hinde, Thomas, 42
Hinton, Daniel, 41
Hippisley (or Hippesley), Edward, 17
Hitchcock (or Hitchcocke), Miles, Capt. Ens. F. reformado Jun 1642, 30; Lieut. F. under Thomas Grantham Sep 1642, 44
Hoare, ___, Lieut. F. under Lord Saye, Sep 1642, 40. Possibly the man below, as two other officers of Lord Saye's were also listed under Bamfield in June.
Hoare, Thomas, Lieut. F. to Christopher Burgh under William Bamfield, Jun 1642, 40
Hobbey, ___, 55*
Hodges, ___, Capt. F. under Henry Hastings Nov 1642, 55*
Hodges, ___, Capt. F. under John Belasyse Nov 1642, 56*
Hodges, ___, Capt. F. under Sir Charles Lucas Nov 1642, 56*
Hodson, Benjamin, 38
Hodson, John, 14
Hogedon, Ed., 30
Holcroft, Charles, Lieut. F. under Lord Wharton Jun 1642, 24; same, Sep 1642, 40

Holland, John, 16
Holles, Gervase, Maj. F. under Sir Lewis Dyve, list [8] reports as dead, hurt or captured Dec 1642, 62*
Hollis, Denzell, 43
Holloway, ___, 56*
Holman (or Holeman), John, Capt. F. under Henry Wentworth 1640, 13; Maj. F. reformado 1642, 29; Maj. F. under Thomas Grantham Sep 1642, 44
Holtby, Marmaduke, 17
Holyday, ___, 57*
Holyman, Thomas, 38
Homer, ___, 56*
Honiburne, Lancelet, 38
Honyborne, John, 15
Honey, Richard, 38
Honywood, Phillip, 11
Hooke, Benjamin, 41
Hooke, Francis, 20
Hopkinson, John, 44
Horton, Edward, 40. Listed twice in the same regiment: presumably a printing error.
Horton, Jeremy, Lieut. Col. and Ser. Maj. Gen. F. under Lord Wharton, Jun 1642, 24; Lieut. Col. F. under Lord Wharton Sep 1642, 40
Horton, Thomas, 50
Hoskins, John, Lieut. F. under Earl of Newport 1640, 10; Lieut. F. under Lord Mandeville Sep 1642, 42
Hotham, John, 49
Howard, ___, Lieut. Col. F. under Sir Charles Vavasour 1640, 16
Howard, Neptune, Ens. F. under Lord Barrymore 1640, 13
Howard, William, Lieut. F. under Lord Saye, Sep 1642, 40
Huddleston, Henry, 20
Hudson, Francis, 41
Hudson, Robert, Commander of fire ship *Swan* Apr 1643, 68
Hudson, Thomas, Quart. H. under Lord Broghill Jun 1642, 23
Hudson, Thomas, Ens. F. under William Bamfield Sep 1642, 44
Huet – *see also* Hewet
Huet, ___, 56*
Hugganes, Robert, 17
Hughes, John, 45
Hughes, Nicholas, 17
Hughes, Robert, Ens. F. under Lord Wharton Jun 1642, 24; Ens. F. under same, Sep 1642, 40
Hulstone, Edward, 17
Huncks, Hercules, 19
Hunt, Edward, 31
Hunt, John, Ens. F. under Jerom Brett 1640, 21
Hunt, John, Quart. F. under Lord Brooke Sep 1642, 42

Hunt, Robert, 43
Hunt, Thomas, 21
Hunter, William, 42
Huntingdon, Ferdinando Hastings 6th Earl of, 35
Hurry, Alexander, 42
Hurry, John, 23
Hussey, ___, 57*
Hutchinson, George, Maj. F. under William Bamfield, Jun 1642, 26; Lieut. Col. F. under Lord Saye Sep 1642, 40
Hutton, George, 49
Hutton, Phillip, 16
Hyde (or Hide), Jo., Cor. H. under John Trenchard Jun 1642, 24; Lieut. under Ch__ Chichester Sep 1642, 51
Hyde, William, 23
Ingoldsbie, Richard, 46
Irby, Sir Anthony, 53
Iremonger, John, 17
Ireton, Henry, 51
Isaack, __, 56*
Ivey, Jo., 24
Jackson, ___, Capt. F. under Sir Thomas Glemham Nov 1642, 55*
Jackson, Edward, Ens. F. under Earl of Northumberland 1640, 10
Jackson, John, Capt. H. under Duke of York Dec 1642, 61*
Jackson, Richard, Ens. under William Bamfield Sep 1642, 43
James, John, 51
Janes, Joseph, 51
Jaques, Joseph, 29
Jefford, John, 17
Jeftres, James, 10
Jenings, Edward, 42
Jenkins, Henry, 43
Jenkins, Jo., 45
Jennings, Ambrose, 21
Jepson, Norrice, 21
Jervas (or Jervis), John, Ens. F. under Sir James Hamilton 1640, 20; Capt. Ens. F. reformado 1642, 30
Jesop, John, Capt. F. under William Bamfield Sep 1642, 43
Jesopp, John, Gentleman of the Ordnance reformado Jun 1642, 31
Jewks – *see also* Jukes
Jewks, Thomas, 48
Jewty, William, 47
Jinkins, John, 26
Jobson, Michael, 43
Johnson, ___, Captain F. under Henry Hastings Nov 1642, 55*
Johnson, ___, Captain F. under Sir Lewis Dyve Nov 1642, 56*

Johnson, ___, Captain F. under Sir John Gooderick Nov 1642, 56*
Johnson, Bartholomew, Corp. H. under Lord Wharton Jun 1642, 23
Johnson, Edward, Capt. Ens. F. reformado Jun 1642, 30
Johnson, Ed., Lieut. H. under Sir Walter Earle Sep 1642, 50
Johnson, Edward, Capt. of merchant ship *Unicorne* Dec 1642, 34
Johnson, Jo., Ens. F. under Earl of Essex Sep 1642, 38
Jolly, Richard, 48
Joans, Thomas, Capt. of merchant ship *Anne and Joyce* Apr 1643, 68
Jones, ___, Capt. F. under Sir Edward Osborne Nov 1642, 57*
Jones, Francis, Capt. Ens. F. reformado Jun 1642, 30
Jones, Henry, Preacher to Richard Feilding's regiment 1640, 13
Jones, Humphrey, Capt. F. under Sir William Constable Sep 1642, 44
Jones, Richard, Col. Capt. F. reformado Jun 1642, 30
Jones, Richard, Capt. F. under Sir Henry Cholmley Sep 1642, 43
Jorden, Elias, 34
Jorden (or Jordan), Joseph, Capt. of merchant ship *Pennington* Dec 1642, 34; navy, Capt. of *Expedition* Apr 1643, 68
Joy, Thomas, 41
Jucey, William, 50
Jukes – *see also* Jewkes
Jukes, Bartholomew, 20
Juns, Robert, 20
Justice, Hugh, Ens. F. under Lord Grandison 1640, 12; Capt. Ens. F. reformado Jun 1642, 30; Lieut. F. under Earl of Essex, Sep 1642, 38
Kanyer, Francis, 14
Katcose, Henry, 43
Keckwick, Thomas, 42
Keeling, William, 13
Kellet, Howard, 30
Kelley, ___, Maj. F. under Sir Charles Lucas Nov 1642, 56*; Dec 1642, 60*
Kelly, Jo., 40
Kenarick, Samuel, 45
Kerry, Patrick Fitzmaurice 19th Baron, 'Lord Kerry', Col. F. 24, 31
Kettley, Thomas, 34
Kevison, Samuel, 20
Keyes (or Kayes), Henry, 13
Keyghtley, Silvanus, 20
Kent, Thomas, 12
Kilmurrey (properly Kilmorey), [Robert Needham] 2nd Viscount, Col F. Nov 164, 56*; horse troop Dec 1642, 57*; 60*
King, John, 31
King, Ralph, 17
King, Thomas, 18
Kingstone, Edward, 20
Kingstone, Thomas, 20

Kinsmell (or Kinsman), ___, 16
Kirbie (or Kirkby), Sir Robert, 14
Kirke, Charles, 18
Kirke, Thomas, 11
Kirle, James, 52
Kirle, Robert, Capt. H. Sep 1642, 52
Kirle, Robert, Lieut. H. under John Fleming Sep 1642, 50
Kirton (or Kirten), Posthumus, 10
Knight, Bray, 11
Knight, Paul, 11
Knight, William, 44
Knightley, Edward, 20
Knightley, Robert, 39
Knot, Nicholas, 21
Kowland, John, 11
Kyghley, Edward, 50
Lacy, Richard, 43
Laharn, Thomas, Ens. F. under Earl of Peterborough Sep 1642, 39. There is also a Capt. 'Thomas Lawherne' in the regiment, possibly indicating a list mistake or printing error.
Lambert, George, 18
Lambert, John, navy, Capt. of *Nicodemus* 1640, 22; Commander & Master of *Lilly* Apr 1643, 68
Lamsdie, John, 45
Landen, Edward, 9
Lane, William, 19
Lanford, Thomas, Lieut. F. under Earl of Essex, Sep 1642, 38
Langford, ___, Lieut. F. under Lord Saye, Sep 1642, 40
Langford, Edward, 16
Langford, George, 44
Langham, Thomas, 15
Langley, ___, Lieut. Col. F. under Henry Hastings Nov 1642, 55*
Langley, Francis, Capt. F. under Marquess of Hamilton 1640, 18
Langley, Trinity, Chirurgion to William Vavasour's regiment 1640, 7
Langon, William, 11
Langrish, Hercules, 51
Langton, Christopher, 41
Larrimore, Roger, 9
Latham, Thomas, 9
Latimer, Thomas, Lieut. F. under William Bamfield Jun 1642, 27; same, Sep 1642, 43
Laward, Thomas, Lieut. F. under Sir William Ogle 1640, 18; Capt. F. reformado 1642, 29
Lawday, ___, Lieut. Col. F. under Lord Barrymore 1640, 12
Lawdey, ___, Maj. F. under Sir William Ogle 1640, 18
Lawdy, George, Quart. F. under Earl of Newport 1640, 10

Lawerowyes, Benjamin, 11
Lawherne, Thomas, Capt. F. under Earl of Peterborough Sep 1642, 39. There is also an Ens. 'Thomas Laharn' in the regiment, possibly indicating a list mistake or printing error.
Lawkner, Lewis, 15
Lawrence, Thomas, Lieut. firelocks under Earl of Essex Sep 1642, 39
Lawrence, Thomas, Lieut. F. under Denzell Hollis Sep 1642, 43
Layton – *see also* Leighton
Layton, Titus, Ens. F. under Thomas Lunsford 1640, 17; Lieut. F. reformado Jun 1642, 30
Le Hunt, Sir John, 20
Le Hunt, Richard, 53
Leake, George, 20
Leake, Sir John, 30
Leaman, Edmund, 22
Lee (or Lea), Robert, Capt. of merchant ship *Hopefull Luke* Dec 1642, 34; same, Apr 1643, 68
Lee, Benjamin, Ens. F. under Lord Saye Sep 1642, 40
Lee, Thomas, Lieut. F. reformado Jun 1642, 30; Lieut. under Thomas Grantham Sep 1642, 44
Legg, Richard, Ens. F. under Earl of Newport 1640, 10
Legge, ___, Capt. F. under John Belasyse Nov 1642, 56*
Leigh, Edward, Commander of collier ship *Edward and Elizabeth* Apr 1643, 68
Leigh, George, 13
Leigh, Goddard, 43
Leigh, Hugh, 18
Leigh, Jude, Capt. F. reformado Jun 1642, 29; Capt. F. under Lord Wharton Sep 1642, 40. In the June list Leigh's name was printed as 'Inde': 'I' doubled as 'J', and the 'n' was a common printing error for 'u', where the letter block was accidentally inverted.
Leigh, Richard, 13
Leigh, Thomas, 20
Leighton – *see also* Layton
Leighton, ___, Capt. F. under Sir William Fairfax Sep 1642, 45
Leighton (or Layton), Francis, Capt. F. under William Vavasour 1640, 17
Leighton, Thomas, Capt. F. under Richard Feilding 1640, 13; Maj. F. under Lord Rochford Sep 1642, 41
Leighton, William, Maj. F. under Lord Willoughby (King's Lifeguard), reported dead at Edgehill, 63*
Leventhorp, Ed., Lieut. H. under William St. Leger, Jun 1642, 24; Capt. F. under Earl of Essex Sep 1642, 38
Lever, ___, 56*
Lewis, William, 14
Lewton, ___, 34
Ley, ___, 56*

Licence, Jo., 30
Lidcoat, Richard, 39
Lidcott, Nicholas, 16
Lidcott, Thomas, 50
Lilborne, Jo., 42
Lilbourne, Robert, 48
Lilley, Ralph, 17
Linch, Jo., 44
Lindsey, John, 50
Lindsey, Robert Bertie 1st Earl of, and Lord Great Chamberlain, subscription to levy horse for the King, Jun 1642, 35; Dec 1642, list [8] alleges Lindsey and regiment lost, 58*. *See also* Lord Willoughby, 2nd Earl of Lindsey (acceded after father's death at Edgehill).
Ling, Carax, 49
Ling, Nicholas, 42
Lisle (or Lesley), George, Capt. F. under Lord Grandison 1640, 12; list [8] reports as dead, hurt or captured, Dec 1642, 62*. It also names Lisle as Lieut. Col. to Thomas Blague: although the rank is correct, at Edgehill Lisle appears to be serving independently with the dragoons.
Lisle, George, Quart. F. under Sir William Ogle 1640, 18
Lisle, Francis, 11
Lister, ___, 44
Little, George, 19
Littleton, Edward, 1st Baron Lyttleton, confirmed as having sided with the King Dec 1642, 65
Llewellin, William, 45
Lloyd – *see also* Floyd
Lloyd (or Floyd), Broichel, 14
Lloyd (or Fludd), Charles, 9
Lloyd, Jeffery, 41
Lloyd, John, Lieut. F. under Sir John Merrick 1640, 15; Capt. F. under same, Sep 1642, 39
Lloyd, John, Ens. F. under Earl of Essex Sep 1642, 38
Lloyd, John, Ens. F. under Sir William Fairfax Sep 1642, 45
Lloyd, Walter, 40
Lloyde, Richard, 11
Lock, Gedeon, 23
Loftus, Sam., Capt. F. under Charles Essex Jun 1642, 26; same, Sep 1642, 46
Loftus, Thomas, 50
Long, ___, Capt. F. under Sir Thomas Glemham Nov 1642, 55*
Long, Robert, Capt. F. under Lord Wharton Jun 1642, 24; same, Sep 1642, 40
Long, Walter, Capt. H. Sep 1642, 51
Longueville, Sir Edward, 1st Baronet, confirmed as having sided with the King Dec 1642, 65
Lookar, Jo., Lieut. F. under Thomas Ballard Jun 1642, 25; same, Sep 1642, 45

Lord Keeper, Edward Littleton, 1st Baron Lyttelton, 35
Louch, Edward, 16
Lovejoy, Caleb, 44
Lovelace, Hugh, 20
Lovelace, John 2nd Baron Lovelace, subscription to levy horse for the King, Jun 1642, 36; confirmed as having sided with the King Dec 1642, 65
Lovell, Edward, 41
Lovell, Henry, Capt. F. under Earl of Peterborough Sep 1642, 39
Lovell, Henry, Ens. F. under Lord St. John Sep 1642, 41
Lovellis, Richard, 11
Lowe, Arthur, 17
Lowe, Laurence, Chirurgion to the Earl of Northumberland's regiment 1640, 10; 'Chirurgion to the Traine and Person' to the Earl of Essex, 1642, 39
Lower, ___, Capt. F. under Sir John Merrick, Sep 1642, 39
Lower, George, Lieut. F. under Earl of Newport 1640, 10
Lower, George, Lieut. F. to Daniel Goodrick under Lord Kerry Jun 1642, 25
Lower, George, Capt. F. reformado Jun 1642, 30
Lower, William, Lieut. F. under Sir Jacob Astley 1640, 11; Capt. F. under Lord Kerry Jun 1642, 25; Maj. F. under Thomas Ballard Sep 1642, 45
Lowes, Phillip, 13
Lucas, Richard, Capt. of merchant ship *Exchange* Dec 1642, 34; same, Apr 1643, 68
Lucas, Sir Charles, Col. F. Nov 1642, 56*. This entry in the November list is indisputably wrong, as Lucas never commanded foot. Many colonels did command both, and perhaps Lucas was provisionally named as being one, although nothing ever came of it. Horse troop Nov 1642, 57*; Dec 1642, 60*; Maj. H. under Earl of Carnarvon Dec 1642, 61*
Lucas, Robert, Provost Marshall to Lord St. John's regiment Sep 1642, 41
Luch, Ithiell, 19
Lucy, ___, 56*
Ludlow, Benjamin, Provost Master to Thomas Ballard Jun 1642, 31; Provost Marshall to same, Sep 1642, 45
Ludlow, Robert, 30
Lukin (or Lukine), Isaac, 13
Lunsford (or Lonsford), Harbert, 17
Lunsford (or Lonsford), Henry, 17
Lunsford (or Lonsford), Sir Thomas, Col. F. 1640, 17; reported captured at Edgehill, 63*
Lure, John, 22
Luther, John, 15
Lutterell, John, 10
Lutton, James, Capt. of merchant ship *Maydenhead* Apr 1643, 68
Lutton (or Lutten), William, navy, Lieut. of *Convertine* 1640, 22; Lieut. of *Rainbow* Dec 1642, 33
Lycent, John, 20
Lyon, Daniell, 53

Lyon, John, 37
Lyster, Thomas, 16
Lyeathcock, Humphrey, 42
Madox, David, 47, 48
Mainwaring, Sir Henry, 22
Maleroy, Averoy, 16
Mallery, Robert, 40
Mallowes, Samuel, 16
Malorye, John, 12
Malten, George, 50
Manaton, Samuel (or Samson), Ens. F. under William Bamfield Jun 1642, 27; same, Sep 1642, 43
Mandeville, Henry Montagu 1st Earl of Manchester, Col. F. Sep 1642, 42. The entry is possibly incorrect, as at the time of the list's publication Henry Montagu was 1st Earl of Manchester and his son Edward used the courtesy title Viscount Mandeville. Edward succeeded his father as earl in November 1642 and became a prominent Parliamentarian.
Maning, Richard, 31
Manly, Robert, 30
Manwarring, Andrew, 25
Manwood, Jeremy, 21
Marine, Robert, 53
Marrow, George, 40
Marly, John, 11
Marsh, Robert, 10
Marshall, John, Lieut. F. under Sir Nicholas Byron 1640, 19; Lieut. F. reformado 1642, 30
Marshall, Jo. Ens. F. under Lord St. John Sep 1642, 41
Marshall, Jo., Corp. H. under Sir Faithful Fortescue Jun 1642, 23
Marshall, Steven, 39
Marshin, Henry, 12
Martery, Useus, 39
Martin, Francis, Capt. F. under Thomas Lunsford 1640, 17
Martin, Francis, Maj. F. under Thomas Ballard Jun 1642, 25; same, Sep 1642, 45
Martin, George, Capt. of merchant ship *Martin* Dec 1642, 33; same, Apr 1643, 68
Marwood, James, 16
Masham, Anthony, Capt. Ens. F. reformado Jun 1642, 30; Lieut. F. under Lord Wharton, Sep 1642, 40
Mason, Richard, 16
Massy (or Massie), Edward, Capt. F. under Philip Wharton, Jun 1642, 24; Lieut. Col. F. under Earl of Stamford Sep 1642, 40
Masters, George, 16
Mathewes, Henry, 21
Mathewes, Humphrey, 29
Mathews, William, 15

Mathias, Christopher, 38
Mattersey, John, 42
Matthewes, Simon, 47
Maunder, Richard, 48
Maxwell, ___, Capt. F. under William Vavasour 1640, 17
Maxwell, Edward, Quart. H. reformado 1642, 29
May, Roger, 20
May, Thomas, 19
May (or Maxy), William, 15
Maylard, Edward, 18
Meautas, Philip, 25
Meldram, John, 47
Melson, Edward, 41
Melvin, John, 42
Menns, Andrew, 11
Menns, Sir John, navy, *Rainbow* Dec 1642, 33
Mercer, John, 42
Mercer, William, 23
Meredith, John, 17
Merick, Gelly, 15
Merrick, Francis, 39
Merrick, John, Ens. F. under Lord Robartes Sep 1642, 42
Merricke (or Mirick), Sir John, Col. F. 1640, 15; Col. F. 1642, 39; 46
Mesham, Thomas, 48
Metoo, ___, 56*
Mewer, Nicholas, 53
Mewer, Robert, 53
Mewer, Thomas, 53
Midehoope, J___, 51
Middleton, John, Capt. F. under Sir Nicholas Byron 1640, 19
Middleton, John, Ens. F. under Thomas Grantham Sep 1642, 44
Middleton, Thomas, Capt. F. under Sir John Dougless, 20
Middleton, Thomas, Capt. F. under Thomas Ballard Jun 1642, 25; same, Sep 1642, 45
Milbourn, Math., 42
Mildmay, J___, navy, Commander & Master of *Revenge*, attendant on the fleet, Apr 1643, 67
Milemay (usu. Mildmay), Anthony, 50
Milemay (usu. Mildmay), Henry, 'of Graces', 51
Milemay (usu. Mildmay), Robert, 51
Miles, Thomas, 41
Mill, John, 42
Millard, John, 11
Miller, Henry, Ens. F. under Earl of Northumberland 1640, 10
Miller, Henry, Preacher to Sir James Hamilton's regiment 1640, 20
Miller, William, 44

Mills, Francis, 17
Mills, Henry, 30
Milshaw, Thomas, 15
Minn, Thomas, 13
Minshaw, Jo., Lieut. F. under William Bamfield Jun 1642, 26; Capt. F. under same Sep 1642, 43
Mintridge, William, 15
Mohun, William, 16
Mohun, Warwick 2nd Baron Mohun of Okehampton, 36
Molineux, Sir Vivian, 20
Molineux, William, 14
Molleneux, Prestland, 30
Mollineaux (or Molleneux), Thomas, Lieut. F. under Jerom Brett 1640, 20; Lieut. F. reformado 1642, 30
Mollineux, Roger, 19
Molworth, Edward, 16
Momford, Peter, 45
Monck, Arthur, 10
Monck, George, 10
Monings, William, 45
Monmouth, Henry Carey 2nd Earl of, subscription to levy horse for the King, Jun 1642, 36; confirmed as having sided with the King Dec 1642, 65
Monyngs (or Monnings), William, 18
More, Daniel, 11
Morgan, Miles, 48, 52 (troop appears twice in the list)
Moore, Francis, 18
Moore, James, Lieut. H. reformado Jun 1642, 30; Lieut. H. under Francis Fines Sep 1642, 50
Moore, Richard, Quart. H. reformado Jun 1642, 29
Moore, Richard, Lieut. F. under Lord St. John Sep 1642, 41
Moore, Roger, Ens. F. under Lord Wharton Jun 1642, 24; same, Sep 1642, 40
Moore, William, Lieut. F. under Earl of Northumberland 1640, 9
Moore, William, Quart. F. under Sir Thomas Glemham 1640, 14
Mordent, Lewis, 41
Morgan, ___, Capt. F. under Lord Grandison Nov 1642, 56*
Morgan, James, Capt. F. under Sir Nicholas Byron 1640, 19
Morgan, Thomas, Capt. of merchant ship *James Youghall* Apr 1643, 68
Morris, ___, 46
Morris, John, navy, Capt. of *Saint George* 1640, 22
Morris, John, Lieut. F. under Lord Brooke Sep 1642, 42
Morton, Leonard, Ens. F. under Thomas Ballard Jun 1642, 25; Lieut. under same, Sep 1642, 45
Mosley, Thomas, 49
Moulsworth, Guy, Lieut. F. under Earl of Northumberland, 9; Lieut. Col. F. under Lord Viscount Cromwell, Dec 1642, 60*

Moulton, Robert, navy, Capt. of *Swiftsure* Apr 1643, 67

Mountague, Francis Browne 3rd Viscount, 36

Mountros, ___, Lieut. Col. F. to the Lord General. list [8] reports as dead, hurt or captured Dec 1642, 62*

Mowbray, Henry Frederick Howard, 15th Baron Mowbray, subscription to levy horse for the King, Jun 1642, 36; confirmed as having sided with King Dec 1642, 65

Moyer (or Mover), Laurence, Capt. of merchant ship *Hurclens* Dec 1642, 34; Capt. of *Hercules* Apr 1643, 68

Moyle, Nathanael, 13; Maj. F., list [8] reports as dead, hurt or captured Dec 1642, 62*. The pamphlet incorrectly states that Moyle was Maj. to Richard Bolle; in fact, it was to Thomas Lunsford.

Muggridge, ___, 56*

Munington, Richard, 19

Murrey, ___, Lieut. Col. F. under John Belasyse Nov 1642, 56*; Dec 1642, 60*

Murrey (or Murray), Sir David, navy, Capt. of *Rainbow* 1640, 22; Capt. of *Reformation* Dec 1642, 33

Murrian, Ralph, 21

Muschamp, Agmondisham, 25

Musgrave, ___, Capt. F. under Lord Grandison Nov 1642, 56*

Musgrave, John, Capt. Ens. reformado Jun 1642, 30

Musket, Fulk, 38

Mynn, Robert, 14

Mynne (or Myn), John, Ens. F. under Richard Feilding 1640, 13; Capt. Ens. F. reformado 1642, 30

Mynne, Nicholas, 17

Napper, Sheldon, 44

Narrow, George, 26

Naupham, Richard, 20

Nayerne, Thomas, 25

Nayrne (or Nerne), Alexander, Capt. H. Jun 1642, 23; Capt. Dr. under James Wardlaw Sep 1642, 53

Neal, John, 49

Neale, Emanuel, 19

Neale, Moses, 44

Neale, Noah, 41

Neale, Timothy, 41

Neale, Walter, 11

Needham, Atwell, 45

Needham, Simon, 44

Nelson, Edward, 11

Nelson, John, 29

Nelson, Robert, Ens. to Richard Feilding 1640, 13

Nelson, Robert, Ens. to William Bamfield 1642, 26

Neve, Edward, 43

Neve, William, 14

Index 113

Newark, Henry Pierrepoint Viscount Newark (son of 1st Earl of Kingston-upon-Hull), subscription to levy horse for the King, Jun 1642, 36; Dec 1642, 62*; confirmed as having sided with the King Dec 1642, 65
Newcastle, William Cavendish 1st Earl of, Col. F. Nov 1642, 55*; Dec 1642, 60*; confirmed as having sided with the King Dec 1642, 65
Newcombe, Jonathan, Lieut. F. under Lord Saye, Sep 1642, 40
Newcomin, John, navy, Lieut. of *James* 1640, 22
Newdigate, Henry, 41
Newdigate, Richard, 48
Newport, Mountjoy Blunt 1st Earl of 1640, 10; 1642, subscription to levy horse for the King, Jun 1642, 36; confirmed as having sided with the King Dec 1642, 65
Newton, John, 10
Nicholas, Sir Edward, 36
Nicholas, Robert, 17
Nicholls, ___, Capt. F. under Sir Thomas Culpepper 1640, 15
Nicholls, ___, Capt. F. under William Vavasour 1640, 17
Nicholls, ___, Capt. F. under John Hampden Sep 1642, 46
Nicholls, Daniell, Lieut. F. under Sir Thomas Culpepper 1640, 16
Nicholls, Humfry, Capt. F. under Jerom Brett 1640, 20
Noard, Roger, 43
Norbury, Edward, Lieut. F. under Thomas Ballard Jun 1642, 25; same, Sep 1642, 45
Norcott, William, 13
Normington, Jos., 42
Norris, Phillip, 14
Norship, Jo., 41
North, John, Commander of collier ship *Recovery* Apr 1643, 68
Northampton, Spencer Compton 2nd Earl of, subscription to levy horse for the King, Jun 1642, 35; foot regiment, Dec 1642, 60*; horse troop under Duke of York, 61*; Dec 1642, 62*; confirmed as having sided with the King Dec 1642, 65
Northumberland, Algernon Percy 10th Earl of, 9
Norton, ___, 34
Norwood, Richard, 14
Noyes (or Noyce), Robert, Lieut. F. under Thomas Ballard Jun 1642, 25; Capt. F. under same, Sep 1642, 45
Noyse, Robert, Lieut. F. under George Goring 1640, 11
Nuby, Henry, 51
Nurford, Peter, 25
Oakes, George, 21
Oakley (or Okely), Edward, 'Battery Master and elder Mate to the Master Gunner', reformado, Jun 1642, 31; Battery Master, Sep 1642, 38
Odingsells (or Ondingsell), Edward, Lieut. F. under Thomas Ballard Jun 1642, 25; Capt. under Sir William Fairfax Sep 1642, 45
Ogee, William, 45
Ogle, ___, Maj. F. under Sir Thomas Culpepper 1640, 15
Ogle, Edward, Ens. F. under Sir William Ogle 1640, 18

Ogle, Gerrard, Ens. F. under Sir William Ogle 1640, 18
Ogle, James, Capt. F. under Francis Hamond 1640, 21
Ogle, Thomas, Maj. F. under Charles Essex Jun 1642, 26
Ogle, Sir William, Col. F. 1640, 18
Okey, John, 48
Oneale (or Oneile), Brien, Maj. under Sir Edward Osborne, 57*; 1642, 60*
Oneyle, Daniel, Maj. H. under Prince Rupert Dec 1642, 61*
Orfice, Richard, 39
Osborne, Sir Edward, Col. F. Nov 1642, 57*; Dec 1642, 60*
Osborne, Richard, Ens. F. under Earl of Essex Jun 1642, 26
Otter, Edward, 45
Otter, John, 49
Ousby, Robert, 42
Outman, Anthony, 31
Owen, ___, navy, Capt. of *Entrance* Dec 1642, 33
Owen, ___, Capt. F. under Endimion Porter, Nov 1642, 56*
Owen, Jo., Lieut. F. under Denzell Hollis Sep 1642, 43
Owen, Richard, navy, Capt. of *St. George* Apr 1643, 67
Owen, Thomas, Lieut. F. under William Vavasour 1640, 17
Owen, Walter, Capt. F. under Sir Thomas Culpepper 1640, 15; Capt. F. reformado 1642, 29
Owen, William, Ens. F. under Sir John Merrick 1640, 15
Owen, William, Capt. F. under William Bamfield Sep 1642, 43
Owens, Owen, 10
Owens, Thomas, 13
Oxenbridge, Charles, 13
Oxenden, Richard, 21
Oxford, ___, Ens. F. under Sir Jacob Astley 1640, 11
Oxford, Wendy, Lieut. F. under Lord St. John 1642, 41
Page, Jo., 41
Paget, William 5th Baron, 36
Pagett (or Padgit), Thomas, 17
Paleologus (or Palealogus, Paholigus), Theodore, Lieut. F. under Sir Jacob Astley 1640, 11; Col. Capt. F. reformado Jun 1642, 30; Lieut. F. under Lord St. John Sep 1642, 41
Palmer, ___, Chirurgion to Sir Thomas Glemham's regiment 1640, 14
Palmer, Giles, 16
Palmer, John, Lieut. F. under Jerom Brett 1640, 20
Palmer, John, Cor. H. under Earl of Bedford Sep 1642, 47
Palmer, Peter, 50
Palmer, Robert, 42
Palmer, William, Lieut. F. under Earl of Northumberland 1640, 9
Paramore, Thomas, Ens. F. under Earl of Newport 1640, 10
Paramour, Thomas, Ens. F. under Charles Essex 1642, 26
Pargiter, Arthur, 44

Parin, Robert, 48
Parker, Charles, Ens. F. under Thomas Ballard Jun 1642, 25; same, Sep 1642, 45
Parker, Henry, 37
Parker, John, 10
Parker, Nicholas, 20
Parker, Richard, Lieut. F. under Sir Thomas Culpepper 1640, 16; Capt. Ens. F. reformado 1642, 30
Parker, Richard, Lieut. F. under Denzell Hollis Sep 1642, 43
Parker, Richard, Ens. F. under Lord St. John Sep 1642, 41
Parkes, William, 39
Parkinson, Jo., Capt. F. reformado Jun 1642, 29
Parkinson, Jo., Lieut. Col. F. under Viscount Mandeville Sep 1642, 42
Parramore, ___, Capt. F. under Earl of Northumberland 1640, 9
Parrimore, Thomas, Ens. F. under Earl of Northumberland 1640, 10
Parris, Jo., 30
Parry, Owen, Capt. F. under Lord Wentworth 1640, 14,
Parry, Owen, Maj. F. under Lord Wharton Jun 1642, 24; same, Sep 1642, 40
Parsell, Garret, 12
Partridge, ___, 34
Pate, ___, 16
Paterson, William, 19
Patrick, William, 53
Pawlet, ___, Capt. F. under William Bamfield Sep 1642, 44
Pawlet (or Poulett), John 1st Baron Pawlet of Hinton St. George, subscription to levy horse for the King, Jun 1642, 36; confirmed as having sided with the King Dec 1642, 65
Pawlet, Sir John, Lieut. Col. F. under Sir Thomas Glemham 1640, 14
Pawlett, Thomas, Ens. F. under Sir Thomas Glemham 1640, 14
Pawlett, William, Lieut. F. under Sir Thomas Glemham 1640, 14
Payard, Alexander, 43
Payne (or Paine), Jervais (or Jarvis), Capt. F. under Marquess of Hamilton 1640, 18; Maj. F. under Sir William Fairfax Sep 1642, 45
Payton, Sir Edward, 39
Payton, Henry, 12
Payton, Samuel, 15
Peacocke, James, Commander of collier ship *Dragon* Apr 1643, 68
Pearne, Jo., 23
Pedar, Matthew, 52
Pemberton, Godard, 19
Pemberton, Lewis, Capt. Ens. F. reformado Jun 1642, 30; Capt. F. under Lord St. John Sep 1642, 41
Pennington, Sir John, 22
Pennyman, Sir William, Col. F., horse troop under Duke of York mentioned Dec 1642, 61*
Pereont, Edward, 14

Pergent, Thomas, 19
Perkins (or Pirkins), Robert, 14
Persall, Charles, 21
Peterborough, John Mordaunt 1st Earl of, General of the Ordnance, Sep 1642, 37; Col. F., 39; Capt. H., 47
Peters, Benjamin, Capt. of merchant ship *Speedwell* Apr 1643, 68
Peters, Henry, 19
Peto, Sir Edward, 41
Peto, Henry, 19
Peto, Jo., 42
Pettus, Thomas, 20
Pew, John, Ens. F. under Earl of Peterborough 1642, 39. There is also an Ens. 'John Apew' ('Ap Hugh'?) listed in the regiment, suggesting a list error or printing mistake.
Pheasant, Thomas, 12
Phenix, George, 30
Philips, Hugh, 43
Phillips, Chichester, 29
Phillips, John, 18
Phillips, Richard, 40
Philpot, John, 21
Phipp, Nicholas, 24
Phipps, John, 37
Pie (usu. Pye), Sir Robert, 52
Piggit (or Pigot), Sir Thomas, Capt. F. reformado Jun 1642, 29; Capt. F. under Thomas Grantham Sep 1642, 44
Piggot, Jo., Capt. of merchant ship *Mayflower* Apr 1643, 68
Pike, Henry, 21
Pilkington, Lyon, 41
Pincock, William, 40
Pitches, Lambert, Commander of fire ship *Sarah* Apr 1643, 68
Plomer, ___, 21
Ploughman (or Plowman), Mathew, Lieut. F. under Francis Hamond 1640, 21; Lieut. H. under William Pretty Sep 1642, 48, 52 (troop appears twice in list).
Pluncket, Thomas navy, Commander & Master of *Cressent* Apr 1643, 68
Pollard, ___, 56*
Pollocke, John, 30
Pomeroy, Hugh, Ens. F. under Sir Jacob Astley 1640, 11
Pomeroy, Hugh, Capt. F. under Thomas Lunsford 1640, 17
Pomroy, ___, Lieut. of merchant ship *London* Dec 1642, 34
Poore, Francis, 20
Poore, John, 41
Pope, ___, 56*
Popham, Edward, 22
Porter, Endimion, Col. F. Nov 1642, 56*; Dec 1642, 60*

Porter, Giles, 9

Povey, Allen, Lieut. F. under Thomas Lunsford 1640, 17; Lieut. F. to Horatio Carey under William Bamfield Jun 1642, 26; Capt. F. under Denzell Hollis Sep 1642, 43

Povey, John, 22

Powell, ___, Maj. F. under Thomas Lunsford 1640, 17

Powell, Edward, 17

Powell, James, Capt. F. under Sir John Dougless 1640, 20

Powell, James, Capt. F. reformado 1640, 30

Powell, John, 29

Powell, Robert, 40

Powell, Roger, Maj. F. under Sir John Gooderick Nov 1642, 56*; Dec 1642, 60*

Powell, Walter, 30

Powell, William, Provost Marshall to Sir Charles Vavasour's regiment, 16

Power, Miles, 12

Pownall, Henry, 44

Predeaux (or Preddocks), William, 11

Predeux, Benil, 31

Prenton, John, 19

Pretty, William, Capt. H. under Lord Grandison 1640, 12; Capt. H. reformado 1642, 29; Capt. H. Sep 1642, 48, 52. Pretty's troop is duplicated in the September list, appearing as no. 17 and no. 70; the latter has a different quartermaster.

Price, Sir Herbert Col. F., Dec 1642, 60*

Price, John, 43

Price, Lodowicke, 12

Price, Richard, 38

Price, Sam., Capt. F. under William Bamfield Jun 1642, 26; Maj. F. under same, Sep 1642, 43

Price (or Prisse), Thomas, navy, Capt. of *Mary Rose* 1640, 22; Capt. of *Lyon* 1642, 33.

Price, Walter, 19

Prideaux, Bevill, 39

Prideaux, Prue, 40

Primrose, Edward, Capt. F. under Thomas Ballard Jun 1642, 25; same, Sep 1642, 45. The earlier list does not give Primrose's first name.

Prior, Bennett, 19

Prowse, ___, 56*

Pudsey, Edward, 48

Pudsey, Marmaduke, 30

Purfoy, George, 25

Purpell, Robert, 45

Purpitt, Edward, 20

Purvey, Denny, 21

Pym, Alexander, 49

Quarls, James, 43

Radford, Thomas, 40
Radley, Sir Henry, Capt. F., reported captured at Edgehill, 63*
Ragan, Cornelius, 18
Rainborow, Thomas, navy, Capt. of *Swallow* Apr 1643, 67
Rainsford, John, Lieut. F. under Earl of Essex, Sep 1642, 38
Rainsford, John, Lieut. F. under Lord Saye, Sep 1642, 40
Ramsey, Jo., 42
Ramsford, Jo., Lieut. F. to Henry Shelley under Lord Kerry Jun 1642, 25. Possibly one of the 'Rainsford' individuals above.
Ransom, George, 38
Raven, Miles, 31
Rawlins, ___, 11
Rawlins, William, Quart. F. to Thomas Ballard's regiment Jun 1642, 31; Quart. F. to Lord Robartes' regiment Sep 1642, 43
Rawson, Thomas, 38
Raymant, ___, 46
Raymond, Jo., 25
Read, John, 45
Read, Richard, 20
Redman, Daniel, Ens. F. under Sir Nicholas Byron 1640, 19
Redman, Daniel, Capt. F. under Lord Mandeville Sep 1642, 42
Redman, Daniel, Lieut. F. under Lord Kerry Jun 1642, 25; Lieut. F. under Thomas Ballard Sep 1642, 45. Redman's first name is not given in the June list, but there he is Lieut. to William Lower, who also appears under Ballard in September, making it virtually certain that these Redman individuals are the same man.
Reed, Walter, 38
Regnolds, James, 29
Reevs, William, 19
Reston, William, 30
Reyley, Henry, 14
Rice, John, Lieut. F. under Earl of Peterborough, Sep 1642, 39
Rice, John, Chirurgion to Earl of Stamford's regiment, Sep 1642, 40
Rich, ___, Lieut. Col. F. under Earl of Newcastle Nov 1642, 55*
Rich, Robert, Baron Rich of Leighs, 'Lord Rich' (son of Robert Rich, 2nd Earl of Warwick), subscription to levy horse for the King, Jun 1642, 36; horse troop Nov 1642, 57*; confirmed as having sided with the King Dec 1642, 65
Richardson, Christopher, 31
Richardson, Thomas, 37
Richardson, William 20
Richmond, James Stuart 1st Duke of, subscription to levy horse for the King, Jun 1642, 35; confirmed as having sided with the King Dec 1642, 65
Ridgley, ___, 56*
Rivers, John Savage 2nd Earl, 36
Roberts, ___, Capt. F. under Sir Thomas Culpepper 1640, 15

Roberts, Arthur, Capt. F. under Francis Hamond 1640, 21
Roberts, Edward, Ens. F. under Henry Wentworth 1640, 14
Roberts (usu. Robartes), John 2nd Baron, Col. F. Sep 1642, 42
Roberts, Thomas, Ens. F. under Lord Brook Sep 1642, 41
Roberts, William, Capt. F. under Henry Wentworth 1640, 14
Roberts, William, Capt. F. under Charles Essex Jun 1642, 26; same, Sep 1642, 45
Roberts, William, 'Fire-worker and Petardier' Sep 1642, 38
Roberts, William, Chirurgion to Lord St. John's regiment Sep 1642, 41
Robinson, Daniel, Lieut. F. under Jerom Brett 1640, 20
Robinson, Daniel, Lieut. F. under Charles Essex Sep 1642, 46
Robinson, Jo., 30
Rochester, John, Capt. of merchant ship *Exchange* Apr 1643, 68
Rochford, John Carey 2nd Viscount, 'Lord Rochford' (son of Henry Carey, 1st Earl of Dover), 41
Rocke, John, 13
Rockwell, Thomas, 22
Rockwood, Thomas, 20
Rodes, Sir John, 55*
Roe, Henry, 38
Roe, Thomas, 44
Rogers, ___, 19
Rogers, Francis, Ens. F. under Richard Feilding 1640, 21
Rogers, Francis, Capt. F. under Sir William Fairfax Sep 1642, 45
Rogers, Thomas, Capt. F. reformado Jun 1642, 29; Capt. F. under Thomas Grantham Sep 1642, 44
Rolson, William, 21
Romitree, Ralph, 49
Rooke, Ambrose, 49
Rookes, Robert, 14
Rookes, Thomas, 20; Capt. Ens. F. reformado 1642, 30
Rookwood, Hogan, 43
Rose, Jo., Ens. F. under William Bamfield Jun 1642, 26; same, Sep 1642, 43
Rose, Jo., Lieut. F. under Lord Mandeville Sep 1642, 42
Rosington, Robert, 13
Ross, William, 20
Roston, William, 13
Rotheram, George, 43
Rouse, George, Lieut. F. under Marquess of Hamilton 1640, 19; Lieut. F. under Earl of Peterborough 1642, 39
Rouse, Thomas, 42
Rowse, Edward, 29
Rudgley, Symon, 53
Prince Rupert, General of H., Nov 164, 57*; horse regiment Dec 1642, 61*
Rush, Thomas, Lieut. F. under Sir Nicholas Byron 1640, 19; Lieut. F. reformado Jun 1642, 30; Capt. F. under Sir William Fairfax Sep 1642, 45

Russell, ___, Lieut. Col. F. under Sir Francis Wortley Nov 1642, 55*
Russell, John, Lieut. F. under Lord Barrymore 1640, 12
Russell (or Rushell), Robert, Capt. F. under Sir Jacob Astley 1640, 11
Ruston, Robert, 21
Rutton, Thomas, 45
St. John (or St. Johns), ___, Capt. F. under Sir Jacob Astley, 1640, 10
St. John, Sir Anthony, Capt. under Earl of Essex 1642, 38
St. John (or St. Johns), Howard, Capt. F. under Marquess of Hamilton 1640, 19
St. John, John, 'Physitian to the Train and Person' to the Earl of Essex, Sep 1642, 39
St. John, Oliver, 5th Baron St. John of Bletso, 'Lord St. John', Col. F. Sep 1642, 41; Capt. H., 48
St. John, Oliver, Ens. F. to Henry Skipwith under Earl of Essex 1642, 24
St. Leger (or Sleger), Rowland, 15
St. Leger, William, 24
Salisbury, William Cecil 2nd Earl of, confirmed as having sided with the King Dec 1642, 65. Salisbury's inclusion is not entirely correct, as he was not at Oxford and remained more-or-less neutral; he suffered materially as a result.
Salkeld, John, 10
Sambridge, ___, 42
Samuel, ___, 43
Sanbedge, John, 17
Sanders (or Sanders), Edward, Col. Capt. H. reformado Jun 1642, 30; Lieut. Capt. H. under Edward Berry Sep 1642, 50
Sanders, Sir John, 52
Sanders, Mount, 41
Sanders, Pilemon, 17
Sanders, Thomas, 14
Sanderson, Henry, Lieut. H. reformado Jun 1642, 29; Lieut. H. under Franci Dowett Sep 1642, 49
Sanderson, Montague, 10
Sandford, ___, Capt. F. under Earl of Northumberland 1640, 9
Sandford, Thomas, Quart. F. under Earl of Northumberland 1640, 10
Sandys (or Sands), Edwin, 47, 50
Sandys (or Sandes), Robert, 18
Savage, ___, Lieut. Col. under Sir Edward Osborne Nov 1642, 57*; Dec 1642, 60*
Savill, Thomas 2nd Baron Savile of Pontefract, subscription to levy horse for the King, Jun 1642, 36; Dec 1642, 62*; confirmed as having sided with the King Dec 1642, 65
Savill, Thomas, Capt. F. under Earl of Stamford Sep 1642, 40
Saye and Sele, William Fiennes 8th Baron, 'Lord Saye', Col. F. Sep 1642, 40; Capt. H., 48
Sayer, ___, 49
Scanderith, John, 16
Scarborough, Jos., 41
Scober (or Scooler), Paul, Quart. H. reformado Jun 1642, 29; Quart. H. under Sir

Walter Earle Sep 1642, 50
Scott, Robert, 21
Scroope, Adrian, 51
Scudamore, ___, 16
Scudamore, Barnaby, Maj. F., list [8] reports as dead, hurt or captured Dec 1642, 62*. The pamphlet incorrectly states that Scudamore was Maj. to Thomas Blague; in fact, it was to Henry Hastings.
Searle, Richard, 44
Sears, Jos., 41
Sedescue, ___, 23
Sedgwick, William, 44
Seigneur, James, 37
Selwin (or Selvin), Sir Nicholas, 10
Seymor, William, Baron Seymour, 'Lord Seymor' (son of William Seymour, 2nd Duke of Somerset)? Identification uncertain. Confirmed as having sided with the King Dec 1642, 65
Seymour (or Seymer), Edward, 15
Seymour (or Symoure), Thomas, 18
Shaftoe, Thomas, Capt. of merchant ship *Blessing* Apr 1643, 68
Shancks (or Shanke), Jo., Capt. Ens. F. reformado Jun 1642, 30; Lieut. F. under Sir Henry Cholmley Sep 1642, 43
Sharpe, Francis, 49
Shawbury, Isaac, 21
Shawe, William, 41
Sheffield, James, 48
Shelley (or Sully), Henry, Capt. F. under George Goring 1640, 11
Shelley, Henry, Lieut. Col. F. under Lord Kerry 1642, 24
Shelton, ___, Capt. F. under Sir Francis Wortley Nov 1642, 55*
Shelton (or Sheldon), Thomas, Capt. F. under Earl of Newport 1640, 10
Shelton, Thomas, Ens. under Sir James Hamilton 1640, 20
Shelton, Thomas, Capt. H. under Duke of York Dec 1642, 61*
Sheppard, Jo., 41
Sherborne, Stafford, 13
Shergall, Robert, 46
Sherley, Thomas, Capt. F. under Sir Nicholas Byron 1640, 19; Lieut. Col. F. under Sir Lewis Dyve, list [8] reports as dead, hurt or captured Dec 1642, 62*
Sherman, John, 16
Sherwood, Christian, 17
Sherwood, William, 31
Shilling, Sheerly, 19
Shipman, Abraham, 19
Shipman, John, Ens. F. under Sir Nicholas Byron 1640, 19
Shipman, Jo., Ens. F. under Charles Essex 1642, 26; same, Sep 1642, 45
Shuttleworth, Nicholas, 29
Sibthorp, Henry, 12

Simpson, William, 20
Sing, Josua, Provost Master to Charles Essex's regiment, reformado, Jun 1642, 32; Gentleman of the Ordnance, Sep 1642, 38
Sippence, Thomas, 38
Skerrew, Robert, 17
Skinner, Thomas, 38
Skippon, Philip, 37
Skipwith, Henry, Capt. F. under Lord Wharton Jun 1642, 24; same, Sep 1642, 40
Skipwith, John, 13
Skipwith, William, 30
Skrimpshiere, Jo., Capt. F. under Earl of Essex Sep 1642, 38
Skrimshaw, Herald, 43
Skrimshawe (or Shrumshaw), Charles, Capt. F. under Sir John Merrick 1640, 15
Skrynsheere, ___, Cor. H. under William St. Leger Jun 1642, 24
Skudamore, John, 42
Slatford, George, Lieut. F. under Sir Jacob Astley 1640, 11; Capt. F. under Thomas Grantham Sep 1642, 44
Slaughter, John, 19
Sleigh, James, 45
Slingsby, ___, navy, Capt. of *Garland* Dec 1642, 33
Slingsby, ___, navy, Lieut. of *James* Dec 1642, 33
Slingsby, ___, Captain F. under Sir Lewis Dyve Nov 1642, 55*; Dec 1642, 58*
Slingsbey, Arthur, 22
Slingsbey, Robert, 22
Sloconil, Humfry, 20
Smart, ___, Capt. F. under Sir Thomas Glemham Nov 1642, 55*
Smart, Tracey, Ens. under Earl of Essex Sep 1642, 45
Smelomb, Barnard, 42
Smith, Francis, 12
Smith, Henry, 41
Smith, John, Wagon Master to Lord Brooke's regiment Sep 1642, 42
Smith, Sir John, Capt. H., Dec 1642, 60*
Smith, Joseph, 44
Smith, Nathanael, 16
Smith, Nicholas, Quart. H. under William Pretty Sep 1642, 48. Pretty's troop is duplicated in the list: in the other instance, a different officer appears as quartermaster.
Smith, Paul, 18
Smith, Richard, 19
Smith, Robert, 13
Smith, Thomas, 15
Smith, William, Lieut. F. under Lord Grandison 1640, 12
Smith, William, navy, Lieut. of *Leopard* 1640, 22; Lieut. of *Saint George* Dec 1642, 33; Capt. of *Lyon* Apr 1643, 68
Smithwick, Francis, 14

Somerster (or Sommerstar, Samerster), Henry, Lieut. F. under Sir Jacob Astley 1640, 11; Lieut. F. reformado Jun 1642, 30; Capt. F. under Lord Mandeville Sep 1642, 42
Sommerston (or Soamaster), ___, navy, Lieut. of *Unicorne* Dec 1642, 33; Capt. of *Dreadnought* Apr 1643, 67
Song, Jenkin, 38
Southampton, Thomas Wriothesley, 4th Earl of, subscription to levy horse for the King, Jun 1642, 35; Dec 1642, 62*; confirmed as having sided with the King Dec 1642, 65
Southcot, Thomas, 43
Sparkes, Ralph, 12
Sparrow, Thomas, 44
Spooner, John, 42
Spoore, Richard, 13
Spry, William, Lieut. F. reformado Jun 1642, 30; Lieut. H. under Thomas Terrill Sep 1642, 51
Spurstow, William, 46
Stafferton, Thomas, 44
Stafford, ___, 55*
Stamford, ___, Cor. H. to Sir John Digby under Lord Grandison, 'of Warwickshire', Dec 1642, 60*
Stamford, Henry Grey 1st Earl of, Col. F. Sep 1642, 40; Capt. H., 48
Stanbury, ___, Capt. F. under Henry Wentworth 1640, 14
Stanbury, Thomas, Lieut. F. under Henry Wentworth 1640, 14
Standburgh (Standbury?), Humfrey, Ens. F. under Henry Wentworth 1640, 14
Standsbury (or Stansbey, Stanesby), John, navy, Lieut. of *Rainbow* 1640, 22; Dec 1642, 33; Capt. of *Converteine* Apr 1643, 67
Stanhope, ___, 56*
Stanley, ___, Maj. F. under Henry Hastings Nov 1642, 55*; Dec 1642, 60*
Stanley, ___, Lieut. Col. F. under Sir Charles Lucas Nov 1642, 56*; Dec 1642, 60*
Stannard, William, 42
Stansby, ___, Capt. of merchant ship *Joslyn* Apr 1643, 68
Staples, George, 23
Stapleton, Sir Philip, 39
Starkeley, ___, 55*
Starkey, Jo., Corp. H. under John Trenchard, Jun 1642, 24
Starkey, Jo., Ens. F. under Earl of Stamford, Sep 1642, 40
Steed, John, 16
Stenchion, James, 53
Stephens, John, 33
Stepkin, Charles, 12
Stevens, Henry, 38
Stevens, Richard, Lieut. H. reformado 1642, 29
Stevens, Richard, Quart. H. reformado 1642, 29
Stevens, Trestram, navy, 'of Dover', Capt. of *Charles* Apr 1643, 67

Steward, Henry, 29
Stiles, John, 46
Stoaker, Matth., 41
Story, ___, Capt. F. under Sir Thomas Glemham 1640, 14
Story, Francis, Maj. F. under Sir James Hamilton 1640, 19
Strading, Sir Edward Col. F. reported captured at Edgehill, 63*
Stradling, Francis, 19
Stradling, Henry, navy, Capt. of *Convertine* 1640, 22; Capt. *Bonny Venture* 1642, 34
Stradling, John, 10
Stradling, Robert, 50
Strange, James Stanley, Lord Strange, confirmed as having sided with the King Dec 1642, 65. Stanley used the courtesy title 'Lord Strange' until his father's death in September 1642, after which he succeeded him as 7th Earl of Derby. The author of list [9], in December, was probably not yet aware that Stanley's transition from Lord to Earl had taken place.
Strangewayes, ___, Capt. H. under Sir Charles Lucas Nov 1642, 56*
Strangeways, James, Cor. H. under Sir Lewis Dyve, reported dead at Edgehill, 63*
Stratford, William, Ens. F. under Sir James Hamilton 1640, 20; same under Charles Essex Sep 1642, 45
Strelley (or Strelly), John, 39, 49
Strelley, Patrick, 38
Strelly, Henry, 48
Stringer, Jacob, Lieut. F. under Sir Thomas Glemham 1640, 14; Ens. F. to Charles Dawson under Lord Kerry Jun 1642, 25; Lieut. F. under Sir William Constable Sep 1642, 44
Strong (or Stroung), Peter, Capt. of merchant ship *Peter* Dec 1642, 34; same, Apr 1643, 69
Struice, Elias, Capt. firelocks under Lord Wharton Jun 1642, 24; Capt. F. under same, Sep 1642, 40
Sumner, ___, 44
Sutton, ___, ___ F. under Sir John Gooderick Nov 1642, 56*
Sutton, John, Lieut. F. under Richard Feilding 1640, 21
Swaine, William, 14
Swan, William, 11
Swanley, ___, navy, Capt. of *Charles* Dec 1642, 33
Swanley, Richard, navy, Capt. of *Leopard* 1640, 22; Capt. of *Bonadventure* Apr 1643, 68
Swanley (or Swandly), William, Capt. of merchant ship *Providence* Dec 1642, 34; same, Apr 1643, 68
Swanly, George, Capt. of merchant ship *Bonny Venter* Dec 1642, 34
Sweeper, Thomas, 40
Swinford, Thomas, 21
Swright [*sic*], James, 47
Taaffe, Theobald 2nd Viscount Taaffe, 'Lord Taaffe', Col. F. 55*; Dec 1642, 58*
Talbot, John, 21
Tapper, Nathaniel, 40

Tasburgh, Peregrine, 11
Taton, William, 42
Tayler, Henry, 41
Tempest, ___, 56*
Temple, James, Capt. F. under Lord Saye Sep 1642, 40
Temple, James, Capt. H. Sep 1642, 49
Temple, Thomas, Capt. H. reformado Jun 1642, 29; Capt. H. Sep 1642, 52
Terrill, Thomas, 51
Terwhit, John, 11
Tetlow, Edward, 44
Thanet, John Tufton 2nd Earl of, subscription to levy horse for the King, Jun 1642, 36; confirmed as having sided with the King Dec 1642, 65
Thelwell (or Thilwill), Anthony, Capt. F. under Richard Feilding 1640, 13; Maj. under same 1640, 21
Thirlow, ___, 56*
Thomas, ___, Capt. F. under Viscount Kilmurrey Nov 1642, 56*
Thomas, Henry, Capt. F. under Richard Feilding 1640, 13
Thomas, John, Ens. F. under Henry Wentworth 1640, 14
Thomas, John, Capt. of merchant ship *John* Dec 1642, 34
Thomas, William, navy, Capt. of *Eighth Whelp* Apr 1643, 67
Thompson, ___, Preacher to Sir Charles Vavasour's regiment 1640, 16
Thompson, Charles, 11
Thompson, Francis, Capt. H. Sep 1642, 52
Thompson, George, 49
Thompson, Richard, navy, Master of ketch *Prosperous*, attendant on the fleet, Apr 1643, 67
Thomson, James, 13
Thory, Alexander, 39
Thornehill, Richard, 46
Thornton (or Therneton), ___, 16
Thorogood, Thomas, 41
Thorp, William, 39
Thorpe, Anthony, 16
Throckmorton, Henry, 44
Throckmorton, Job, 44
Throgmorton, Nicholas, 29
Throgmorton, Thomas, 11
Throughton, Isaac, 14
Throughwood, Thomas, 19
Throwley, Ed., 51
Thurland, Richard, 15
Thwaytes, Thomas, 15
Tindall, Ambrose, Lieut. F. under Sir John Merrick 1640, 15; Lieut. F. to William Roberts under Charles Essex Jun 1642, 26; Capt. firelocks to Earl of Essex Sep 1642, 39

Tinne (or Tinney), Morgan, Lieut. F. to Herbert Blankchard under Lord Kerry, Jun 1642, 25; Capt. F. under Lord Saye, Sep 1642, 40
Tirringham, Francis, 21
Tirwhit – *see also* Tyrwhit
Tirwhit, Edward, 21
Tirwhit, Francis, 21
Tirwhit, George, 45
Tirwhit, John, 21
Tisdale, ___, 56*
Tooke, James, 21
Tooley, John, 9
Tomkins, William, 13
Tovey, William, Quart. H. reformado Jun 1642, 29; Quart. H. under Lord Feilding, Sep 1642, 48
Townsend, Robert, 10
Townsend, Thomas, 20
Trafford, Thomas, Capt. F. under Lord Barrymore 1640, 12
Trafford, Thomas, Capt. F. under Lord Taaffe, Dec 1642, 58*
Travers, Richard, 21
Treadwell, Moses (or Treswell, Moyses), Lieut. F. under Marquess of Hamilton 1640, 19; Capt. F. reformado 1642, 29
Treist, Thomas, 39
Treme, John, 39
Trenchard, John, 24
Treveere, Thomas, 55*
Trevor (or Trever), Daniel, Lieut. F. under Sir Nicholas Byron 1640, 19; Lieut. F. under Lord Robartes Sep 1642, 42
Troughton, Christopher, 38
Trunke, William, 45
Tucker, ___, 39
Tuke (or Tucke), William, Lieut. F. under Marquess of Hamilton 1640, 19; Capt. Ens. F. reformado 1642, 30
Tukes, ___, 55*
Tulidaffe, Alexander, 42
Turbervill, Troibus, 29
Turkington, ___, 42
Turner, ___, Provost Marshall to Sir Thomas Culpepper's regiment 1640, 16
Turner, Francis, Capt. F. reformado Jun 1642, 30
Turner, John, Provost Marshall to Lord Mandeville's regiment Sep 1640, 42. Possibly the unnamed man above.
Turner, Robert, Lieut. F. reformado Jun 1642, 30
Turner, Robert, Capt. firelocks to Earl of Essex Sep 1642, 39
Turner, Thomas, navy, *Swiftsure* 1640, 22
Turney, Isaac, 40
Turrell, Thomas, 42

Turvill, Poole, 21
Turvill, Robert, 15
Tyerer (or Tyrer, Tyer), Edward, Lieut. F. under Francis Hamond 1640, 21; Lieut. F. to Vincent Calmady under Lord Wharton Jun 1642, 24; Capt. F. to same, Sep 1642, 39
Tyrer, Thomas, 45
Tyrwhit – *see also* Tirwhit
Tyrwhit, ___, Lieut. Col. F. under William Vavasour 1640, 16
Ugall, Henry, 16
Upton, ___, 55*
Upton, John, 49
Upton, Richard, 45
Urrey, John, 47
Usher, George, 40
Usher, James, Maj. F. under Lord Barrymore 1640, 12
Usher, James, Capt. F. reformado 1642, 29
Uvedale (or Udall), Sir William, 10
Vaines, Thomas, 31
Vanbraham, H__, 50
Vanderhiden, Philip, 24
Vandrusick (usu. Vandrusk), Jonas, 49
Vangerich, Jo., 23
Vanpeere, Henry, 10
Varnon, Thomas, 50
Varvay (or Urney), Edward, 12
Vaughan, ___, Lieut. Col. F. under Henry Hastings Nov 1642, 55*
Vaughan, Thomas, Lieut. F. under Earl of Newport 1640, 10
Vaux, ___, 57*
Vavasour, ___, Lieut. Col. F. under Endimion Porter, Nov 1642, 56*
Vavasour, Sir Charles, Col. F. 1640, 16
Vavasour, William, Col. F. 1640, 16; reported captured at Edgehill, 63*
Vaves, Thomas, 48
Venner, ___, 55*
Ventress, Charles, 20
Ventris, Henry, 18
Vernon, George, 37
Vetty, Max., 51
Vickerman, Ralph, 23
Villiers (or Villars), Edward, 12
Vincent, Edward, 21
Vinter, John, 41
Vittell, John, 21
Vivers, Robert, 52
Wagstaffe (or Wagstaff), [Joseph], Lieut. Col. F. under William Bamfield Jun 1642, 26; same under John Hampden, Sep 1642, 46; Royalist Maj. under Sir Thomas

Glemham Nov 1642, 55*; mentioned by list [8] Dec 1642, 60*. *Mercurius Aulicus* notes his capture and subsequent desertion to the King early in January 1643 (TT E.244[30]), but list [7] was printed early in November, so Wagstaffe's switch must have occurred almost immediately after Edgehill.
Waite (or Wayte), Henry, 13
Waite, John, 18
Wake, Baldwin, navy, Capt. of *Lions Tenth Whelpe* 1640, 22; Capt. of *Expedition* Dec 1642, 33
Walcot, Ralph, 23
Waldegrave (or Walgrave), ___, Capt. F. under Sir Thomas Glemham 1640, 14
Waldegrave, John, Lieut. F. under Sir Thomas Glemham 1640, 14; Capt. F. reformado 1642, 29
Waldron, William, 16
Waldwine, ___, 15
Wales, Charles Prince of, nominal Col. H., subscription to levy horse for the King, Jun 1642, 35; regiment mentioned Dec 1642, 60*
Walker, ___, Capt. to merchant ship *Golden Angel* Dec 1642, 34
Walker, John, Capt. F. under Lord Robartes Sep 1642, 42
Walker, Zachary, Quart. to Lord Kerry's regiment Jun 1642, 31; Quart. H. under Sir Arthur Haselrig Sep 1642, 50
Walkington, Thomas, 21
Waller, ___, Maj. F. under Sir Francis Wortley Nov 1642, 55*
Waller, Sir William, Col. H. Sep 1642, 47, 48
Walley, Edward, 51
Walley, Ellias, 30
Wally, Isaac, 20
Walmesley, Nathaniel, Corp. H. under Alexander Nayrne Jun 1642, 23
Walmsly, Nathaniel; Ens. F. under Lord Mandeville Sep 1642, 42. The unusual name suggests Walmsly is the man above, however this would mean he had switched commander, arm, and rank.
Walset, Ralph, 43
Walsh, George, 41
Walter, George, 44
Walter, Roger, 30
Walters, ___, 33
Walters, John, 12
Walthall, Peter, 19
Walton, ___, 21
Walwin (or Wallen), William, Quart. H. & F. under Lord St. John Sep 1642, 41, 48
Wanderford, Michael, 50
Warburton, Richard, 31
Ward, Andrew, 38
Ward, Arthur, 14
Ward, Henry, Lieut. F. reformado Jun 1642, 30
Ward, Henry, Carriage Master to Sir William Fairfax's regiment Sep 1642, 45

Ward, Hugh, 47
Ward, John, 37
Ward, Thomas, Lieut. F. under Sir Thomas Glemham, 1640, 14
Ward, Thomas, Capt. F. reformado Jun 1642, 30; Capt. F. under Earl of Essex, Sep 1642, 38
Wardlaw (or Wardlo), James, 53
Wardlaw, Sir William, 46
Wardley, William, 52
Ware, Peter, Cor. H. under Lord Wharton Jun 1642, 23; same, Sep 1642, 48
Warren, ___, 11
Warren, Henry, 10
Warren, John, 41
Warren, Nicholas, 42
Warson, George, 21
Warwick, Robert Rich 2nd Earl of, navy, *James* Dec 1642, 33; *Prince Royall* Apr 1643, 67
Wase, Edward, 'Under Conductor of the Amunition, and traine of Artillery', reformado, Jun 1642, 31; Gentleman of the Ordnance, Sep 1642, 38
Wase, Roger, 46
Washer, ___, 56*
Washington, Henry, Capt. F. under Earl of Northumberland 1640, 9; Lieut. Col. F. under Sir John Gooderick Nov 1642, 56*; Dec 1642, 60*
Washington, John, 10
Waterhouse, Jos., 52
Waters, ___, 55*
Watham, Robert, 19
Watkins, Jo., Ens. F. under Charles Essex Jun 1642, 26; same, Sep 1642, 45
Wats, Paul, 25
Watson, ___, Capt. F. under Marquess of Hamilton 1640, 19
Watson, Nicholas, Ens. F. under Sir Nicholas Byron 1640, 19
Wattes, ___, 33
Watton, ___, Cor. H. under Valentine Walton Sep 1642, 52
Watton (usu. Walton), Valentine, Capt. H. Sep 1642, 52
Watts, Edward, Lieut. F. under Sir Nicholas Byron 1640, 19; Lieut. F. reformado Jun 1642, 30; Capt. F. under Lord Mandeville Sep 1642, 42
Watts, John, 19
Waynford, ___, 29
Wayte, ___, 26
Webb, James, Lieut. F. under Charles Essex Jun 1642, 26; same, Sep 1642, 45
Weekes, John, Lieut. F. under Earl of Newport 1640, 10
Weekins, Luke, 40
Weeks, ___, Capt. F. under William Ashburnham Nov 1642, 56*
Weeks, Edward, Cor. H. under Ch__ Chichester Sep 1642, 51
Weeler – *see also* Wheeler
Weeler, William, 16

Weild, J__, navy, Commander & Master of *Signet* Apr 1643, 69
Welch, George, 29
Weld, John, 21
Wellin, William, 43
Wells, Samuel, 46
Wentworth, George, 38
Wentworth, Henry, 13
Wentworth, William, 10
West, Edmond, 52
West, Edward, 38
West, George, 51
West, Nathaniel, 48
West, Roger, 30
West, William, 43
Westmorland, Mildmay Fane 2nd Earl of, subscription to levy horse for the King, Jun 1642, 36; horse troop under Duke of York, Dec 1642, 61*; confirmed as having sided with the King, 65
Weston, William, 12
Wett, Edward, 45
Wharton, Philip, 4th Baron Wharton, 'Lord Wharton', Col. General, Jun 1642, 24, 31; Col. F. Sep 1642, 40; Capt. H., 48
Wheathill, Gilbert, 14
Wheeler – *see also* Weeler
Wheeler, Abraham, navy, Capt. of *Greyhound* 1640, 22; same, Dec 1642, 33; same, Apr 1643, 67
Wheeler, John, 45
Wheeler, Oliver, 30
Wheeler, Simon, 32
Whetstone, Roger, 42
Whistler, Ralfe, Capt. H. under Lord Wharton Jun 1642, 23; Lieut. H. under same, Sep 1642, 48
Whitbread, Jo., 51
White, ___, Capt. F. under Lord Taaffe Nov 1642, 55*
White, ___, Capt. F. under Endimion Porter Nov 1642, 56*
White, ___, Lieutenant, arm not given, reported dead at Edgehill, 63*
White, George, Capt. F. under Lord Barrymore 1640, 12
White, John, Ens. F. under Sir William Fairfax Sep 1642, 45
White, Peter, navy, Commander & Master of *Nottordam*, attendant on the fleet, Apr 1643, 67
White, William, Lieut. F. under Earl of Stamford Sep 1642, 40
Whiteacre, ___, 55*
Whiteaway, ___, 56*
Whitley, Matthew, 14
Whitney, Francis, 21
Whitney, Thomas, 45

Index

Whymper, Richard, 23
Wilkinson, Smith, 43
Willeby, ___, 33
Willet, John, 31
Willet, Roger, 30
Willet, Theodore, 30
Willey, Theophilus, 45
Williams, ___, Capt. F. under Endimion Porter, Nov 1642, 56*
Williams, Anthony, Ens. F. under Marquess of Hamilton 1640, 19
Williams, Hugh, Lieut. F. under Henry Wentworth 1640, 14
Williams, Osmond (or Osborn), Lieut. F. reformado Jun 1642, 30; Capt. F. under Lord Mandeville Sep 1642, 42
Williams, Ralph, Lieut. F. under Earl of Essex Sep 1642, 45
Williams, Thomas, Lieut. pioneers Sep 1642, 38
Williams, William, Ens. F. under Lord Rochford Sep 1642, 41
Willier, Francis, 19
Willins, Ralph, 31
Willis, Rawley, 43
Willis, Richard, Maj. F. under George Goring 1640, 11; Maj. H. under Lord Grandison, Dec 1642, 60*; same, Dec 1642, 61*; reported dead at Edgehill, 63*
Willoughby, ___, Maj. F. under Lord Grandison Nov 1642, 55*
Willoughby, Montagu Bertie, Lord Willoughby de Eresby; became 2nd Earl of Lindsey after his father's death at Edgehill. Subscription to levy horse for the King, Jun 1642, 36; horse troops Nov 1642, 57*; horse troop under Duke of York Dec 1642, 61*; Dec 1642, 62*; reported captured at Edgehill, 63*; confirmed as having sided with the King Dec 1642, 65
Willoughby, Francis, 5th Baron Willoughby of Parham, 47, 48
Willoughby, George, Capt. F. under Lord Rochford Sep 1642, 41
Willoughby, Robert, Ens. F. under Denzell Hollis Sep 1642, 43
Wilmot, Henry, Commissary Generall H. and Col. H., regiment mentioned Dec 1642, 61*
Wilsheere, Jo., 30
Wilson, Fenix, 17
Wilson, Francis, Capt. F. reformado Jun 1642, 29; Capt. F. under Lord Mandeville Sep 1642, 42
Wiltshire (or Wilshiere, Wilsheere), Robert, Lieut. F. under Lord Grandison 1640, 12; Lieut. F. reformado Jun 1642, 30; Capt. F. under Sir William Fairfax Sep 1642, 45
Winchester, Alexander, 50
Windfeild, John, 21
Windham, George, 20
Windsor, Frederick, 14
Wingate, Edward, 51
Wingfield, George, 43
Wingfield (or Winckfield), Sir Robert, Lieut. Col. F. reformado Jun 1642, 29; Lieut. Col. under William Bamfield Sep 1642, 43

Winter, ___, Capt. F. under Lord Taaffe Nov 1642, 55*
Winter, James, Chirurgion to Sir William Fairfax's regiment Sep 1642, 45
Winter, William, Ens. F. under Sir Nicholas Byron 1640, 19
Witcherly, James, 42
Witherings, Anthony, 18
Withers, ___, Capt. F. under John Belasyse Nov 1642, 56*
Withers, Jo., Ens. F. under Earl of Essex Sep 1642, 45
Withrington, ___, 56*
Wivell, ___, 42
Wolverstone, John, 19
Wood, Edward, 30
Wood, J___, navy, Commander & Master of *Nichodemus* Apr 1643, 67
Wood, John, 41
Wood, Nicholas, 42
Wood, Robert, 24
Woodhouse, ___, Dec 1642, 60*
Woodman, Christopher, 21
Woodnorth (or Woodnoth), Henry, Cor. H. reformado Jun 1642, 29; Quart. H. under Edward Berry Sep 1642, 50
Woodroffe, Foulke, 21
Woods, ___, 15
Woodward, John, 39
Woolward, Anthony, 22
Worsop, John, 21
Worth, Henry, 42
Wortley, Sir Francis, Col. F. Nov 1642, 55*; horse troop, 57*
Wray, Henry, 44
Wray, Sir William, 52
Wren, John, 17
Wren, William, 39
Wright, Gerard, 38
Wright, Samuel, 12
Wright, Vul___, 13
Wroughton, James, 29
Wylde, Thomas, 9
Wynd (or Winde), ___, Capt. F. under Sir Charles Vavasour 1640, 16
Wynd, Robert, Lieut. F. under Lord Grandison 1640, 12
Wythers (or Whither), George, 14
Yarner, John, 44
York, James Duke of, subscription to levy horse for the King, Jun 1642, 35; regiment mentioned, 60*
Young, Arthur, 44